CORE SKILLS

Reading
Comprehension

Harcourt Achieve

Rigby • Steck-Vaughn

www.HarcourtAchieve.com
1.800.531.5015

About the Editor

Donna Loughran is an editor, writer, artist, and multimedia designer living and working in Austin, Texas. She has a B.F.A. in Fine Art and a B.A. in English. She has worked in educational publishing for twelve years.

Acknowledgments

Designer: Julia Hagaman
Cover Design: Alexandra Corona
Interior Illustrations: Donna Loughran
Photography: Donna Loughran

ISBN 0-7398-7039-4
Copyright © 2003 Harcourt Achieve Inc.

Dear Parent,

Welcome to the *Steck-Vaughn Core Skills: Reading Comprehension* series! You have selected a unique book that focuses on developing your child's comprehension skills, the reading and thinking processes associated with the printed word. Because this series was designed with the national standards as a guide, your child will have reading success as well as gain a firm understanding of necessary critical thinking skills.

Reading should be a fun, relaxed activity for children. They should read stories that relate to or build on their own experiences. Vocabulary should be presented in a sequential and logical progression. The stories in this series build on these philosophies to insure your child's reading success. Other important features in this series that will further aid your child include:

- Interesting short reading selections appealing to adolescent readers.

- Vocabulary introduced in context and repeated often.

- Comprehension skills applied in context to make the reading more relevant.

- Multiple choice exercises that develop skills for standardized test taking.

You may wish to have your child read the selections silently or orally, but you will find that sharing the stories and activities with your child will provide additional confidence and support to succeed. When learners experience success, learning becomes a continuous process moving them onward to higher achievements. Moreover, the more your child reads, the more proficient she or he will become.

Enjoy this special time with your child!

Sincerely,
The Educators and Staff of
Steck-Vaughn School Supply

P.S. You might also like to visit the Special Features section of our website at **www.svschoolsupply.com** for other fun activities and learning suggestions.

Contents

Correlation to Language Arts Content Standards

LANGUAGE ARTS SKILLS	PAGE
Comprehension	
Author's Purpose, Audience	42, 88, 111, 118, 119
Cause and Effect	46, 47, 81, 51, 83, 84
Compare and Contrast	59, 60, 61, 62, 82, 90
Drawing Conclusions	30, 37, 45, 46, 47, 54, 61, 103, 104, 106
Fact or Fiction	114, 115
Facts and Inferences	9, 16, 27, 36, 42, 59, 70, 78, 87, 90, 91, 94, 102, 110, 120
Figurative Language	11, 22, 37, 62, 96
Identifying Fact and Opinion	31
Graphic Sources	30, 44, 45, 46, 54, 61, 79, 98, 103, 104, 105, 106, 112, 121
Main Ideas and Supporting Details	20, 48, 49, 51, 71, 92,
Predicting Outcomes	8, 15, 35, 77, 83, 86, 106, 109
Relevant and Irrelevant Information	18, 28
Sequencing	10, 47
Story Elements	9, 17, 27, 36, 42, 47
Vocabulary	
Analogies	63, 97
Antonyms	29, 53
Synonyms	37, 43, 53, 64
Word Meaning	11, 17, 73
Words in Context	43, 74, 82, 97, 117, 121
Research and Study Skills	
Evaluating Persuasive Methods	111, 112, 113, 116, 118, 119
Evaluating Resources	18, 28
Internet and Media Literacy	88, 89, 90
Outlining	21, 72, 95
Skimming	38
Summarizing	10, 52, 60, 81, 119

Mistaken Identity

All kids need friends, especially new kids at Jordan Middle School. My name is Jane Austen Street and I, unfortunately, am one of those new kids. A lot of new kids don't have any trouble fitting in. They make friends fast. But I'm not one of them. I don't usually talk about myself. I've never had an adventure in baby-sitting. I don't wear designer clothes. And, I can never think of just the right thing to say when some kid at school makes me a target of a smart remark. Not that I want to say something smart, you understand. I'm not interested in working hard to be like everybody else. I want to be me, but it takes time. And kids like Madison James just don't get it.

The other day, for example, I wore my overalls to school. I know overalls aren't for everybody, but I like them. Anyway, between classes Madison yells at me in the hall. I'm standing in front of the principal and every eighth-grader at Jordan Middle School when I hear, "Hey, Farmer Street, where's your cow?" I knew I was as red as a late summer tomato because I could feel my face burning. I didn't say anything. Instead, I smiled a pathetic smile and slipped away like I didn't exist.

For the moment, Madison James is my living nightmare. She's the eyelash on my contact. She's the dried blob in my hair gel. She's the…the…well, you get the idea. Ever since I moved across town to Jordan Middle School, Madison has been a pain in my side.

First thing every morning, I look at Madison. She's in Ms. Mitchell's first-period English class just like me. Madison is also the last person I see every day. That's because she and I are in gym last period. She's everywhere I am and everywhere I look. And, she's everything I'm not and everything I don't want to be. She looks like she just stepped out of a magazine. You know what I mean. She's shiny and glossy and, well, together. She's popular and she knows it. She doesn't talk to me unless she has something nasty to say. And she doesn't look at me without squinting. Her eyes practically disappear into hateful lines across her face.

I wasn't surprised when Madison's attention turned to my name. In fact, I was surprised it hadn't happened sooner. Ms. Mitchell started it when she passed out copies of *Pride and Prejudice*. The writer's name is the same as mine—Jane Austen. Obviously, that's not my fault. But as soon as Madison heard the name, she blurted, "Jane Austen? That's your name."

I rolled my eyes, hoping the rest of the class would think that Madison's observation was too obvious, if you know what I mean. "She's my mother's favorite author," I answered casually, pretending that the matter wasn't worth discussing. What I wasn't willing to say was that I like Jane Austen, too. And, so far anyway, *Pride and Prejudice* is my all-time favorite book. I've read it five times already. But there are some things even I know it's smarter to keep to yourself when you're in eighth grade.

Ms. Mitchell explained that Jane Austen lived more than 200 years ago. Madison swung her head around, zeroing in on me like an angry bee with a stinger. "Your mother named you after a dead writer?" A few people in my class snickered. The others seemed struck by boredom.

Almost as a reflex, I said, "I'm named after a dead writer. You're named after a dead president. But you only got his last name." More people seemed to be paying attention this time. I heard more laughter. So did Madison, who looked, probably for the first time in her life, unsure of herself, deflated. She turned around without saying anything.

When I saw Madison's reaction, I felt ashamed. As much as I hated being new and not fitting in right away, I also hated acting like this. My smart remark made me no different than Madison. But I didn't have time to think about it. Ms. Mitchell was giving class assignments.

"I want you to read this book with a partner and confer about it," Ms. Mitchell said. "You have one week. Then, you and your partner will present a short report to the class on a topic that I'll give you today. Madison and Jane," she smiled, looking directly at us, "I want you two to report on what we can learn from the main characters in *Pride and Prejudice.*"

When Ms. Mitchell finished giving assignments, Madison and I took our pass and went to the library. We found a table in the back. Neither of us said anything at first. Then Madison said, "So what's this book about? You must know if you're named after the author."

"Well," I said slowly, "it's about two people who get the wrong idea about each other. One character, Mr. Darcy, is shy. He finds it hard talking to people he doesn't know. Because Mr. Darcy never says anything, Elizabeth Bennet, the other character, thinks he's proud, or stuck up. When Mr. Darcy realizes that Elizabeth has made up her mind about him without getting to know him first, he decides she's prejudiced."

Madison looked at me but didn't say anything right away. Then she smiled a little smile. "So they're wrong about each other," she said.

"Sort of. I mean, Mr. Darcy is a snob and Elizabeth does judge people too quickly. But their ideas about each other are all wrong. It takes them awhile to see each other as they really are." I started feeling nervous as Madison's smile grew larger.

"You mean like us?" she asked. "You acted like you didn't like me from the start. Like you didn't like the way I dress or something."

"That's not it really. You squint at me all the time. And you never stop teasing me," I said.

"Squinting? Oh, that. My mother says that, too. I'm nearsighted, and I don't like to wear my glasses. And my eyes water if I wear contacts. And teasing? I do that with all of my friends. That means I like you."

This time, I was smiling. "Oh, I get it. Then do you think you could like me a little less?"

We both laughed.

"I think I might like reading this book after all," said Madison, squinting at me. "Sounds like the author knows a lot about people."

Suddenly, it hit me. Madison could turn out to be a friend after all.

What happens next?

How do you think Jane and Madison's relationship changed? Write a short paragraph predicting what you think happened in their relationship.

A **Underline the correct answer that completes each statement.**

1. The setting for this story is
   a. a church picnic.
   b. a summer camp.
   c. a middle school.
   d. a high school.

2. Jane is determined to
   a. not be like everyone else.
   b. fit in at all costs.
   c. make the cheerleading team.
   d. wear designer clothes.

3. Jane wears overalls
   a. to annoy Madison.
   b. to do farm chores later.
   c. to be different from the crowd.
   d. to paint after school.

4. To be prejudiced means to
   a. be proud and snobbish.
   b. make judgments without facts.
   c. make precise observations.
   d. be angry and out of sorts.

5. Jane says Madison is her "nightmare" because
   a. Madison copies Jane's test papers.
   b. Madison acts like Jane doesn't exist.
   c. Madison wants Jane to join the debate team.
   d. Madison seems to be everywhere and teases Jane.

6. Madison and Jane are different in that
   a. Madison never thinks of smart remarks.
   b. Madison is popular and dresses like a model.
   c. Madison has never had a baby-sitting adventure.
   d. Madison is quiet and unpopular.

7. The book that Madison and Jane are assigned to read is
   a. *The Baby-Sitters Club.*
   b. *Pride and Prejudice.*
   c. *The Madison Presidency.*
   d. *Sense and Sensibility.*

8. Madison and Jane found out that
   a. they both disliked reading.
   b. their parents knew and liked each other.
   c. each had wrong ideas about the other.
   d. English class can be fun.

B Now, practice summarizing the story. Summarizing, or paraphrasing, helps you understand and remember what you read. It also helps you notice the main idea and important details of the story.

What happened first in the story?

a new girl goes to a new school

What happened next in the story?

she gets tersed by a mean girl

What happened last in the story?

they both become friends

What important lesson did you learn in the story?

don't tease people

C Write the correct word from the Word Box next to each meaning. If you have trouble choosing an answer, look back to the story to see how the word is used.

Word Box

observation	boredom	prejudice
glossy	confer	nearsighted
obvious	snickered	pathetic
snob	deflated	reflex

1. shiny   _____

2. a state of being uninterested   _boredom_____

3. to be unable to see at a distance   _nearsighted_____

4. to arouse pity; to be pitiful   _pathetic_____

5. a judgment formed in spite of facts   _prejudic_____

6. a person who acts superior   _snob_____

7. a conclusion based on looking closely   _observation_____

8. to talk to another about something   _confer_____

9. an unthinking reaction   _reflex_____

10. something very apparent   _obvious_____

11. laughed   _snickered_____

12. acted let down or let the air out of   _deflated_____

D The story uses many similes and metaphors. Remember, a **simile** uses the words *like* or *as* to compare two things. *The dogs ran like the wind.* A **metaphor** does not use the words *like* or *as* to compare two things. *The dog was a clown for the children.* Read the sentences below. Write an **M** next to each metaphor and an **S** next to each simile.

___M___ 1. Madison is the eyelash on my contact.

___S___ 2. I was as red as a late summer tomato.

___M___ 3. Madison is the dried blob in my hair gel.

___M___ 4. Jane is proud as a peacock.

___S___ 5. Madison is like a fashion model.

___S___ 6. Madison James is my living nightmare.

Far Eastern Adventure

I remember listening quietly as my parents talked about our new home in the Far East. It was no surprise to any of us that we were moving again, but no one had expected this to happen. The Air Force was sending us to Okinawa. No one in my family had a clue where Okinawa was until I found the atlas. Together, we searched in Asia, and then among the tiny islands of the Pacific Ocean until we found it. There it was, at the end of a chain of islands below Japan.

Finding the island on a map of the Orient didn't make me feel any better about moving. Our family had already moved three times and I was barely thirteen. I knew I would miss Charlie, my neighbor and best friend. Three years would feel like forever. Charlie and I would be sixteen years old before we saw each other again. But, as the child of an Air Force officer, I had already learned that you have to be flexible.

I should have known that these three years would be unusual. My first clue was the summer we spent in California. There weren't enough houses on Okinawa for families, and we had to wait our turn. Two weeks before my dad left, my parents drove us to an air base in California where we moved into an apartment. Lots of other families were living there, too. There were loads of kids my age. I think half of them belonged to the same family. I loved the Mercer kids. We spent mornings at the base pool and afternoons at the movies, where we could get in for fifty cents. Sometimes our moms drove us all to our favorite park where we'd have picnics and spend the day playing ball and frolicking. Even though I missed Charlie, this summer was moving up on my list of favorite summers.

My second clue that this experience would be different from the others came on the airplane. We had left California and were excited to be on our way to Honolulu, Hawaii. We had to stop there first because the plane couldn't hold enough fuel to get us all the way to Okinawa. I had never been to Hawaii before. I didn't care that we wouldn't be allowed to leave the airport. I was glad to be there and eager to see something. Inside the airport, my mother bought two necklaces of flowers, one for me and one for my little brother. She explained that in Hawaii, people give these necklaces, called leis, as gifts. My lei looked like a beautiful cascading waterfall of white. It was made from dozens of small orchid flowers. I had never had anything like it. I took it off before we got back on the plane. I didn't want to crush the petals. I put the necklace on my lap, which turned out to be a mistake. Hours later, the plane's humming had put me to sleep. However, my brother was wide-awake and looking for something to do. When I opened my eyes again, my necklace was still on my lap. But it didn't have any flowers on it. My brother had picked every petal, leaving me a string. You can imagine what I wanted to do to him.

Eventually, we reached the island. We were going to live on a hill outside the gates of the air base until a house on base became available. We were excited until we saw the hill and the house.

Tall bamboo grass grew up the sides of the hill and alongside the hill's only road. Halfway up, part of the hill had been cut away. That's where our house was. Our house was one of three houses that could fit on the hill. The rest of the space was covered with tombs. We were living next to a cemetery!

At first, I thought my dad couldn't have found a creepier place for us to live, but once I got used to them, the tombs weren't noticeable at all. Then on special holidays, women dressed in beautiful robes came to pray. Sometimes the women left gifts of food outside the tombs. My brother and I knew these days were special, so we stayed indoors, occasionally peeking from a window. The seriousness of the occasion made the people beautiful to watch.

On school days, the bus waited for my brother and me at the bottom of the hill. Then in the afternoon, the bus dropped us off in the same place. Twice each day we walked down and up the hill alongside bamboo that was three times taller than we were. My brother kept his eyes on one side of the road, while I watched the other side. We walked slowly, looking out for the dangerous snakes that we had been told lived in the bamboo forests. Luckily, we never saw one.

In the storm season, when we had warnings of typhoons, my brother and I helped cover the windows in our house with boards. We also helped fill the bathtub, jars, and pots and pans with water. We never knew how long we would have to live without clean water and electricity.

We also never knew what was living in our house with us. We checked closets for snakes and looked inside our shoes before we put them on. Roaches longer than my thumb lived everywhere, even inside the washing machine. It took months for us to find out how they got into our refrigerator. I remember a time when my mom opened the fridge and saw a huge roach walking across her fresh lemon pie. That was the last straw, or I should say, roach. Mom slammed the door shut and went straight to the base to ask for a new refrigerator. It came the next day. The movers took the old refrigerator away and then called later to tell us what they found. An entire roach colony was living in the space between the walls of the refrigerator.

Our family had lots of friends on the island, but just like in California, we found one special family that we visited often. Tony was my age. His sister Sylvia was sixteen. When we were with Sylvia, we listened to music and rehearsed the latest dances. When Tony, my brother, and I were on our own, we searched through the caves behind Tony's house. Late one Sunday afternoon, as we were saying goodbye, the ground began to shake. We froze and watched our car rock back and forth. The car wasn't the only thing rocking. That was my first and only earthquake experience.

I'm lucky. Lots of people take expensive vacations to have the kinds of adventures we had on Okinawa. How many other people get to learn about holidays for the dead, typhoons, poisonous snakes, roaches, and earthquakes without leaving home?

What will happen?

Use clues that you picked up while reading the story to write a short paragraph. Describe what the writer will be like when she grows up. What do you think she will do for a living?

A   **Underline the correct answer to each question.**

1. What important thing happened to the writer of "Far Eastern Adventure"?
   a. She moved to Hawaii for three years.
   b. She stayed in California while her parents went overseas.
   c. She moved with her family to Okinawa for three years.
   d. She was a part of an exchange student program to Germany.

2. What kind of story is this?
   a. how-to paper   b. autobiography
   c. short report   d. persuasive paper

3. Where did the writer look to find out where her family was going?
   a. a travel agency
   b. on the Internet
   c. an atlas
   d. an encyclopedia

4. After looking at a map, where did the writer find she was going?
   a. Hawaii, a U.S. state in the Pacific
   b. California, a U.S. state on the Pacific
   c. Jamaica, an island country in the Caribbean
   d. Okinawa, an island below Japan in the Pacific

5. What was on the hill next to the writer's new home?
   a. tombs
   b. an amusement park
   c. an ornamental garden
   d. a movie theater

6. What kind of plant grew in the forest near the writer's home?
   a. oak trees
   b. bamboo
   c. orchid flowers
   d. palm trees

7. What was living in the refrigerator?
   a. roaches
   b. poisonous snakes
   c. mice
   d. lizards

8. What kind of storms did the writer's family hear about in their new home?
   a. hurricanes   b. monsoons
   c. tornadoes   d. typhoons

B Write the correct word from the Word Box next to each meaning. If you have trouble choosing an answer, look back to the story to see how the word is used.

Word Box

atlas	flexible	bamboo
tomb	noticeable	poisonous
eventually	rehearsed	fantasy
frolicking	typhoon	orchid

---

1. a flower that is made into a necklace _____ *orchid*

2. a collection of maps _____ *atlas*

3. practiced _____ *rehersed*

4. a woody plant that grows in Asia _____ *bamboo*

5. to remain open to change _____ *frolicking*

6. a violent tropical storm or cyclone _____ *typhoon*

7. playing _____ *flexible*

8. something that is hurtful, full of venom _____ *poisonous*

9. an unreal story _____ *fantasy*

10. something that can be seen _____ *noticable*

11. a grave _____ *tomb*

12. in time _____ *eventually*

C Try to answer the questions without looking back at the story.

1. In what hemisphere does the story happen? Northern or Southern?

   _____ *Sothern*

2. In what country does the story happen? _____ *Okinawa*

3. In what ocean is the country located? _____ *Pacifica*

4. In what region does the story happen? Europe? Asia? North America? South America? _____ *Asia*

5. How would you describe the setting or geography of the area?

   _____ *mountainy*

6. What other words are used in the story to name the area the family is in?

   _____

D The girl in the autobiography "Far Eastern Adventure" used an atlas to find out where Okinawa is. What other research tools or experts would have been helpful to her?

1. Underline the sources that the girl and her family can use to find relevant information about the journey.
   a. a library
   b. an air force base
   c. the girl's social studies teacher
   d. an encyclopedia
   e. a dictionary
   f. an Internet search program
   g. a travel agent

2. Which of the sources in question 1 would you use first? Second? Third?

   a f c

3. Circle the letters of four references that might have the most relevant information.
   a. *Japan's Neighbors*
   b. *Travel in China on $50 a Day*
   c. *Atlas of Europe*
   d. Volume "O" of an encyclopedia
   e. the Internet site *www.okinawa.com*
   f. *The Culture and Customs of Japan and Okinawa*
   g. *Ancient Korean Sights*

4. The people listed below have written books. Which three authors would most likely give the relocating air force family relevant information? Underline the answers.
   a. Marcus Grant, a mechanic in California, who services air force planes from Japan
   b. Mr. Yamamoto, a professor of Asian studies at the local community college
   c. Kara Lee, who wrote *A History of the Japanese Islands*
   d. Sandra Walters, who published *Folk Tales From Asia*
   e. Jan Willeke, a former teacher who taught English in Okinawa

Another Kind of Language

Korea is a peninsula below China that juts out into the Sea of Japan. Despite the distance from the United States, many Koreans have come to America to seek their fortune. By 1970, about seventy thousand people of Korean ancestry lived in America. A count of people in 1990 showed that number had increased to almost eight hundred thousand. After the year 2000, the Korean-American population was over one million.

Upon arriving in the United States, Koreans may feel exhausted by trying to make sense of English and the people who speak it. Korean-American families also differ from American families in their definition of what is good behavior. But, because they have a thirst for freedom and a desire for a stable life, they have tried to bridge the wide gap between two very different cultures—Korean and American.

As employers, taxpayers, and consumers, Korean-Americans have helped rebuild many of America's poorer neighborhoods. Because of cultural differences, tensions have developed between residents of these neighborhoods and Korean-Americans. Residents who have lived in these neighborhoods longer resent the changes the Korean-Americans have made. Misunderstandings have occurred between the two groups because of different customs and beliefs about social behavior. Community leaders are trying to get the two groups together to promote understanding.

These differences in culture even extend to differences in body language. Body language is an unspoken language that all cultures have. For example, many Korean-Americans are not as comfortable smiling as Americans are. They believe that if nothing is funny, then there is nothing to smile about. They think it is stupid or foolish to smile without a good reason. So, a smile is not always given upon meeting. Looking someone directly in the eyes is also considered bad manners.

To show affection or to touch in public is considered bad manners in Korean culture, too. A simple gesture, like a man taking a woman's hand, is considered embarrassing. This is why Korean-Americans do not put things, like change, into a person's hand. They usually place the object or money on the counter so that the other person can pick it up without touching.

Each paragraph in "Another Kind of Language" has two or more details that support a main idea. Read the following ideas from the five paragraphs in the story. Label each main idea M. Label each detail D.

Paragraph 1.

_____ Korea is a peninsula that juts out into the Sea of Japan.

_____ Despite the distance, many Koreans have come to America.

_____ After 2000, the Korean-American population was one million.

Paragraph 2.

_____ They may be exhausted by trying to make sense of English.

_____ But, they have tried to bridge the gap between two cultures.

_____ They differ in their beliefs about what is good behavior.

Paragraph 3.

_____ Korean-Americans have rebuilt some poorer neighborhoods.

_____ Tensions have developed because of cultural differences.

_____ Community leaders are trying to get the two groups to talk.

_____ Misunderstandings have occurred.

Paragraph 4.

_____ Korean-Americans are not as comfortable smiling.

_____ These cultural differences extend to body language.

_____ Looking someone directly in the eyes is bad manners.

Paragraph 5.

_____ To show affection or touch in public is bad manners.

_____ They put the change on the counter, without touching.

_____ A simple gesture like holding hands is embarrassing.

Now that you have identified the main ideas and supporting details in the article "Another Kind of Language," it will be easy for you to outline what you learned. Part of the outline has been done for you.

Another Kind of Language

I. Despite distance, many Koreans have come to America.

    A.   Numbers of Korean-Americans have increased over the years.

        1. By 1970, 70,000 people of Korean ancestry lived in the U.S.

        2. _____

        3. _____

    B.   Koreans must make adjustments upon arriving in the U.S.

        1. They must deal with understanding English and English speakers.

        2. _____

        3. _____

           _____

II.   Tensions have developed between Korean-Americans and residents because of cultural differences.

    A.   Korean-Americans have moved in and rebuilt some poor neighborhoods.

        1. People who have lived in neighborhoods longer resent change.

        2. _____

        3. _____

    B.   Differences extend to body language.

        1. _____

        2. _____

        3. _____

           a. Touching hands is considered embarrassing.

           b. They put objects such as change on the counter to avoid touching.

When people begin to learn English, they find that some expressions can be tricky to figure out. These expressions are known as idioms or figurative language.

One young Korean-American student in an ESL class said that a fellow student had told her to "give him a hand with the class science project." At first, she felt a little frightened, because she took his words literally. Of course he later explained that he did not want her hand, but help with the project.

Answer the questions about the meaning of the expressions below.

1. In Japanese culture there is a saying, "the nail that sticks out must be pounded flat." What do you think this might mean if applied to people?

   _____

   _____

2. A Mexican-American saying is, "Don't take off con la cola parada." It can be translated and used as in the following sentence. He heard the news and ran off with his tail flying in the air. What does this mean?

   _____

   _____

3. Sammi looked all over for the machine part and couldn't find it. She thought she had been sent on a wild goose chase. What does it mean if you are sent on a "wild goose chase"?

   _____

   _____

4. Sarah's mom told us that she "had her eye on us." What did she mean?

   _____

   _____

5. A Jamaican, or West Indian, saying is, "Keep on the straight and narrow path." What are you being advised to do?

   _____

   _____

6. The cowboy told his friend, "I feel as low as a snake's belly in a wagon rut." What do you think he was telling his friend?

   _____

   _____

A Trip to Remember

The bus ride from Dallas was the first sign that I wouldn't like Texas. The rocking bus made me sick to my stomach. Plus, the farther I traveled from the airport, the more depressed I felt. I leaned my head against the bus's grimy glass window and watched Texas roll by. The city changed into small towns, which then dissolved into endless flat, brown, dusty fields. I had imagined places like this while I was reading *The Martian Chronicles*. This was Mars, wasn't it? Where were the video arcades, the all-night pizza parlors, the neon lights, the skyscrapers, and the traffic? Modern civilization had disappeared, and I knew I hated Texas!

In a way, this trip started last summer. That was when I met Tyrone at a computer camp in upstate New York. We hit it off from the start, so when he invited me to visit him the next summer, I didn't say no right away. I didn't say yes either, you understand. I had never been outside New York before, and Texas seemed a million miles away. But both my mom and dad thought Tyrone's idea was great. They were all for it. In fact, their exact words were, "The experience will be good for you." At the time, I had no idea what they meant.

Tyrone and his mom met me at the bus depot in San Angelo. I was relieved to see them, but not relieved to learn we still had thirty miles to go in the Peterson's old pick-up truck.

Mrs. Peterson drove the truck down roads dotted with potholes. My head bobbed up and down so hard that I knew if I tried to speak, I'd bite my tongue in half. So I watched silently as the scenery changed from dusty to dustier. Eventually, we turned down a hidden road and into a lane with a barred gate. Tyrone jumped out to open the gate and closed it again after Mrs. Peterson drove through. "We've got lots of animals," he said, pointing proudly to a small herd of horses.

The truck bumped down a deeply rutted track. The truck stopped outside what looked like a soda can on wheels. "Where are we?" I asked Tyrone. He opened the door on the can and announced proudly, "We're home. Come on in."

Tyrone's dad met us at the door. He had dinner ready, and although I didn't recognize the smell, I was starving. Somewhere near the first bite, my eyes watered and I couldn't catch my breath. Tyrone smacked my back, making me spit a mouthful of King Ranch Chicken back on my plate. "This is really good," I said to Mr. Peterson through my tears. The Petersons laughed while I pushed everything that looked like a chili to the edge of my plate. Tyrone seemed to inhale his food, chilis and all.

While I recovered from my near-death experience, Tyrone unpacked for me. It was late and I was worn out. Tyrone could see that I was tired. "I'll wake you up early so we can search for arrowheads before it gets too hot. Sound okay to you?" I nodded and then the lights went out.

The trailer's rocking woke me. Thunder boomed and lightning flashed. In one flash, I looked over at Tyrone—he was sleeping soundly in his bed. Was the rocking of the trailer normal, or should I wake him up to tell him we might wind up in Oz any minute? "New York, I miss you. Texas, I hate you." Those were my last thoughts before I finally fell back into an exhausted sleep.

Early the next morning, Tyrone and I went outside. He had loaned me some denim jeans to wear. The sun was already bright, and the sky was a fresh-washed brilliant blue. I could see clean lines and shapes for miles in every direction. Then I noticed something else. "Tyrone, I don't think I've ever heard so much quiet before." He understood and laughed.

Mrs. Peterson called from the trailer, "Boys, watch out for snakes! Breakfast is almost ready, so come in and wash your hands!"

"Snakes?" I said to Tyrone, stopping in my tracks.

"Yessssssss," he said in a scary voice, "ssssssnakessss. Rattlessssnaakesssssss." What a comedian.

"I hate Texas," I said very quietly under my breath.

After breakfast, we set off with a packed lunch and a hoe to kill any rattlesnakes we might see. I wasn't too happy about the rattlesnake part, but Tyrone said that we might find Indian arrowheads after the rain.

"What kind of Indians were around here?" I asked.

"Lots of different tribes over thousands of years. Comanche, Lipan, Anasazi. We might find something really old."

We reached a gully where Tyrone showed me what flint, the kind of rock the Indians used to chip arrowheads, looked like. He told me, "Head uphill into the sun. Scan the ground and look for anything that catches the light in an unusual way. If you see a rock that looks like it's been worked, pick it up and call me over. If you see or hear a snake, stand still, and call me over."

"Don't worry. I will." At first, it was hard to see so much at once, but after a while, I could spot pieces of flint and chips from arrowheads. By then, even the fear of stepping on a snake had moved to the back of my mind. Hours passed as Tyrone and I moved slowly, inching our way up another bluff. Finally, there it was, lying half in and half out of the sandy ground. I had the feeling that I had been looking at it for several seconds without seeing it. If I had discovered an Egyptian tomb, I couldn't have been more stunned.

"Tyrone, I found one. I found an arrowhead. Wow, a big one."

"Man, that's not just an arrowhead, that's a spear point!"

We started digging. The spearhead was about eight inches long and perfectly formed out of a white translucent flint.

"Wow, let's take it to dad. I bet he'll know what it is. Or, maybe we can go into San Angelo tomorrow to visit old Fort Concho. Experts there know all about Indian artifacts. You can see the Buffalo Soldier exhibit there, too. The Buffalo Soldiers were black soldiers stationed at the fort in the late 1800s. The Comanches gave them the name of Buffalo as a sign of respect because the soldiers were brave."

As we started hiking back to the trailer, I cradled the spear point carefully. The silent beauty of the land struck me as I looked out on a landscape that had been unchanged for perhaps thousands of years. I felt small but important at the same time. There were no crowds of people to blend into, no haze smearing the landscape, no blaring radios or horns. Only me. Only this incredibly bright, quiet, bold land. Maybe Texas wasn't so bad after all.

What will happen?

What do you think will happen when Tyrone goes to visit the author in New York? Write a short paragraph describing Tyrone's first week there.

A **Underline the correct answer to each question.**

1. What is the setting for this autobiography?

   a. a bus on the way to California

   b. a train station in Dallas, Texas

   c. a crowded neighborhood in New York City

   d. a less populated part of West Texas

2. What is the mood in the beginning of the story?

   a. excited   b. joyful

   c. gloomy   d. scary

3. What is the change of heart the writer has in the story?

   a. He decides he likes trailer houses.

   b. He comes to appreciate Texas.

   c. He becomes unafraid of rattlesnakes.

   d. He finds he loves New York City.

4. Where did the writer meet Tyrone?

   a. at computer camp

   b. on a camping trip

   c. on a school trip

   d. on a family vacation

5. Why do you think the writer's parents think the trip will be good for their son?

   a. They know he loves travel to other places.

   b. They want to take a trip of their own.

   c. They think he is a little narrow in his outlook.

   d. They want him to learn more about computers.

6. What did the writer find?

   a. a dinosaur bone

   b. an old well

   c. a buried box of gold

   d. an Indian spear point

7. When does the writer's mood begin to change in the story?

   a. the morning after the rain   b. when he is leaving

   c. the first night   d. when he sees the trailer house

8. Who are the Buffalo soldiers?

   a. characters in a cartoon   b. soldiers stationed in New York City

   c. black soldiers from the 1800s   d. superheroes in a fantasy story

27

B **Tyrone tells the writer of "A Trip to Remember" about the Buffalo Soldiers. Both boys decide they want to find out more about these brave men. Answer the questions below to help point them in the right direction.**

1. Underline the sources the boys can use to find relevant information about the soldiers.

   a. a library

   b. an expert on buffaloes

   c. an African-American artist

   d. an army recruiter's office

   e. an expert at the fort

   f. an Internet search site

   g. an encyclopedia

2. Circle the letters of three references that might have the most relevant information.

   a. *A History of the Army, 1917–2000*

   b. *Traveling Texas Backroads*

   c. *Atlas of Texas*

   d. *Old Fort Concho, a History*

   e. a schedule of bus routes around San Angelo, Texas

   f. *Buffaloes Around the World*

   g. *Famous African-American Military Men*

3. The people listed below have written books. Which three authors would most likely give the boys relevant information? Underline the answers.

   a. Jim Fowland, an animal expert in West Texas

   b. Dr. Marcus Thomas, a professor of African-American studies

   c. Jeff Bullock, who wrote *You're in the Army Now, 1800–1946*

   d. Amy Wong, who wrote *The Architecture of Forts and the People in Them*

   e. Jerry Arredondo, a professor of geography at San Angelo State College

C On each line are two words that are antonyms, or opposite in meaning. Circle the antonyms.

1. united | eroded | dissolved | *disappeared*
2. tractor | skyscraper | *bulldozer* | hut
3. exhibit | *evidence* | *hide* | unashamed
4. *inhale* | reveal | expert | *exhale*
5. *translucent* | pearl | *darkened* | powdery
6. *unafraid* | *prejudiced* | withheld | fair
7. *inflate* | recede | *deflate* | pressure
8. humor | *frolicked* | *sat still* | joyful
9. *noticeable* | blaring | *blends in* | spotted
10. *aloof* | pale | *friendly* | *embarrassed*
11. *depressed* | abrupt | *cheerful* | talkative

D Choose a word from the Word Box to complete each sentence. Some words may not be used.

Word Box

depressed	parlor	neon
arcade	skyscrapers	dissolve
translucent	exhibit	flint
stationed	inhale	comedian
computer	denim	chronicles

1. A special room in a house is a ___denim___.

2. To be funny is to be a ___comedian___.

3. A series of stories or tales are ___chronical___.

4. To be sad or feel down is to be ___depressed___.

5. Something that is clear or lets light show through is ___translucent___.

6. Tall buildings that seem to touch the sky are called ___skyscrapers___.

7. A display or show at a museum is an ___exhibit___.

8. A bright electric light made up of special gases is called ___neon___.

9. To fade or mix into smaller pieces is to ___dissolve___.

10. A video game business is called an ___arcade___.

Look at the illustrations of several kinds of arrowheads and spear points. Notice that they come from different time periods and that they have different styles. Read the text and then underline the correct answer to each question.

The bow and arrow was first used in the Late Prehistoric period, around A.D. 700. Before the bow, darts and lances with large spear points were common. Bird points were probably used to hunt deer and bison since they have been found in remains of those animals. They were also used in battles. More than likely they were not used to hunt birds.

Texas point; mid-1800s

Bird point; from A.D. 700

Stone Age Paleo spear point; probably Anasazi

1. Of the artifacts shown, which is probably the most like the one found in the story "A Trip to Remember"?
   a. Texas point   b. Paleo spear point
   c. not shown   d. bird point

2. Which arrowhead was made closest to the time the Buffalo soldiers were at Fort Concho?
   a. Texas point   b. Paleo spear point
   c. not shown   d. bird point

3. What were bird points thought to have been used for?
   a. hunting flying birds
   b. hunting bison and deer
   c. cleaning hides
   d. grinding corn

4. When were bows and arrows first used?
   a. around the mid-1800s   b. in the Stone Age
   c. around A.D. 700   d. around 1900

5. What was used before the bow and arrow?
   a. Texas points   b. metal tools
   c. bird points   d. darts and lances

When you research a subject, you usually can find many facts about it. Sometimes you may find information that is someone else's opinion. Being able to tell the difference between what is fact and what is opinion is important. Remember, an **opinion** is **a belief or feeling about something**. Now, read an article about an ancient Southwestern Indian culture.

The Anasazi

The Anasazi may be the ancestors of the Pueblo Indian people in New Mexico, Arizona, Colorado, and Utah. They were Stone Age people who did not use any metal or metal tools. They made their tools from stone, wood, and bone. More than likely, they were not as civilized as we are today. The Anasazi made tools for pounding, chopping, hunting, and planting.

The Anasazi started building pueblos about A.D. 700. A pueblo is a village made of stone or clay buildings built next to or stacked on top of one another, sort of like an apartment building. Each family generally had two rooms of a pueblo. They lived in one room and stored food in the other. They probably felt very cramped in their limited indoor surroundings. However, pueblos allowed many people to live in the same area.

All pueblos had kivas. A kiva was a round or square underground room with a roof. People used ladders to climb into kivas. Tunnels connected many kivas. A kiva was used like a church and was a meeting place where the men gathered together to talk.

By the A.D. 1000s, the Anasazi cities were important centers for trade, culture, and learning. But by the 1200s, thousands of Anasazi began to slowly leave their homeland. In less than 100 years, the Anasazi had left behind all they had built. There is some geological evidence to support the idea that a drought, or a time without rain, drove the Anasazi southward into Texas and Mexico. But, perhaps, the Anasazi just grew tired of their environment and decided to move south.

Put an F by each fact from the story and an O by each opinion from the story.

_____ 1. The Anasazi were Stone Age people who did not use any metal or metal tools.

_____ 2. More than likely, the Anasazi were not as civilized as we are today.

_____ 3. The Anasazi started building pueblos about A.D. 700.

_____ 4. Each Anasazi family generally had two rooms of a pueblo.

_____ 5. The Anasazi probably felt very cramped in their limited indoor surroundings.

_____ 6. A kiva was a round or square underground room with a roof.

_____ 7. There is some geological evidence to support the idea that a drought, or a time without rain, drove the Anasazi southward into Texas and Mexico.

_____ 8. But, perhaps, the Anasazi just grew tired of their environment and decided to move south.

Yuki Finds Her Way

The day hadn't started the way Yuki thought it would. She woke feeling tired and grumpy, not the best frame of mind for a ten-mile hike to Blue Hole with the Explorers Club. Then, when she met her best friend, Jada, at the start of the hike, they quarreled about something stupid. Blue Hole was a fantastic place to swim, but Yuki couldn't get excited about walking for hours through thick woods. She struggled to keep up with the others, bringing up the rear of a snaking line of ten other kids led by the club leader, Ms. Reeves.

It was mid-morning when the group stopped for its first water break. Jada sat with some other friends, ignoring Yuki. Yuki felt snubbed and was even more out of sorts. When the group reassembled to resume the hike, Yuki deliberately stayed near the back. "I know this trail," she thought to herself. "I'll take a longer rest and then catch up later." When the last hiker was out of sight, Yuki stretched out at the base of a pine tree. Fingers of sunlight stretched sideways through tree branches to warm her face. Yuki yawned, scrunched down into the roots of the tree, and fell into a deep sleep.

A woodpecker tapped on a branch above Yuki's head, waking her instantly. For a moment, she didn't know where she was. Then Yuki's dry and furry mouth told her that she had slept too long. "What have I done?" Yuki leaped up and started running down the trail. "I've got to catch up!" she thought desperately. Branches and vines clawed and slapped at her as she jogged down the path. Some distance later, Yuki was breathless and felt a vicious thirst. She stopped, holding her aching side with one hand and using the other to fumble through her pack, searching for her half-full water bottle. Despite knowing that she should save some for later, Yuki couldn't stop drinking once the cool water began to trickle over her cracked lips and parched tongue. She stopped drinking when the bottle was dry.

It was then that she felt the raging fire on her face that would undoubtedly cause her skin to blister and peel. The sun must have moved above the trees and baked her while she slept. That meant that she had slept far longer than she had intended. Suddenly, she noticed how long the shadows were. "It must be at least the middle of the afternoon," she thought to herself. The path she was following narrowed to a dark point. "This is a deer trail, not the way to Blue Hole." Fear bubbled up from her belly as she realized her mistake. "I don't know where I am," she whispered to the woods.

Yuki's tears made the forest dip and shimmer, turning it into a runny watercolor of greens and blues. Slowly she tried to retrace her steps, following the slender deer trail. "I have to get back to the place where I slept," she thought desperately. She walked awhile but couldn't find her "sleeping tree." Surely by now Ms. Reeves and the group had come to look for her. Chances were they'd find her before dark. But if they didn't, she'd have to spend the night in the woods.

"Heeelllp! Help me!" yelled Yuki in her panic. "I'm here. Please, I'm over here!"

The woods swallowed her screams, and every other sound, too. There were no buzzing insects, no chirping birds, no scurrying squirrels. She'd never heard such silence before. She'd never felt so alone.

Slowly, a red bird began a sweet song whose notes fell from the tree branches like drops of rain. Joining in, a blue jay scolded, then a bee buzzed by, a squirrel chattered, and a crow cawed. At last, the forest symphony was playing again, and Yuki felt calmer.

She had to get a grip on herself. She couldn't let fear lead her into any more stupid decisions. "Think. Use your head," she said to herself, remembering her grandmother's constant warning to think before acting. "Be an actor, not a reactor," she used to say. There was something else her grandmother used to say. Being positive changes bad luck into good luck. So far today, Yuki thought glumly, she had forgotten everything her grandmother had taught her. Now seemed like a good time to start remembering.

She sat down and ate the last of a leftover breakfast bar. She worked hard to ignore her thirst. She focused instead on trying to determine where she was and from which direction she had come. Then she remembered the reason she had chosen the pine tree where she had slept. It was the tallest tree around, and its top branches were bald.

Yuki drew a line in the forest litter to mark her path as she left the trail to find the nearest outcropping of rocks overlooking the forest. She scanned the forest top, turning in a slow circle. She saw no bald trees peeking above the canopy. She turned again, making herself look calmly at every detail. About a half-mile away, she saw a tall evergreen tree with a bald top crowning thick green limbs. Yuki used her eyes to draw an imaginary line between her sleeping tree and the top of a tree close to the trail. She abandoned the outcrop, heading toward the tree. When she reached it, she stopped and left the trail to scan the woods from another outcropping. There, she took another sighting, drew another imaginary line, and jumped back on the trail. At last, she reached her sleeping tree. Her footprints dented the ground by the rock, and the trail the others had followed that morning was nearby.

There was a chance the kids in the Explorers Club had already come back this way. Yuki got down on her hands and knees, searching the trail for tracks. Small jagged rocks and woody acorns hid beneath dead leaves covering the trail. They punched Yuki's palms and knees as she moved slowly over the ground. Yuki felt the pain but kept moving. The only footprints she found went toward Blue Hole. No one had returned, but that was good news. All she had to do now was wait. She knew she would be in trouble with Ms. Reeves and the club, but she knew that she deserved to be. She also knew that she could have been in much worse trouble if she hadn't started acting instead of reacting. Relief left Yuki almost lighthearted. She went back to the sleeping tree, where she sat in late-afternoon darkness thinking positive thoughts.

Shortly before the sun said goodnight, Yuki heard the welcome sound of voices. Her grandmother was right again.

What might have happened?

Think about what you have learned about Yuki. Write a paragraph to describe what you think might have happened if Yuki hadn't been rescued that same day.

Underline the correct answer to each question.

1. What is the setting of this story?
   a. a bamboo forest with mountains
   b. a pine forest with trails and rock outcroppings
   c. an oak forest with a wide river
   d. a grassy plain with a deep gorge

2. What were Yuki's reasons for staying behind?
   a. She wanted to wait for a different group of explorers.
   b. She was following a beautiful butterfly that had landed on her sleeve.
   c. She awoke tired and in a bad mood, and she argued with her friend.
   d. She had turned her ankle and needed to keep off of it.

3. How did Yuki get lost?
   a. She read the wrong map.
   b. She stayed behind and took a nap.
   c. She followed the wrong group of explorers.
   d. She wandered into an old mine.

4. What is the author's purpose for using descriptive language like "vicious thirst"?
   a. The author wants to show off her vocabulary.
   b. The descriptions are there to take up space on the page.
   c. The author wants to improve the reader's vocabulary.
   d. The descriptions help the reader experience what Yuki is feeling.

5. What helped Yuki calm down and begin to think?
   a. She had a cup of hot tea from her thermos.
   b. She began to breathe deeply.
   c. She remembered her grandmother's advice.
   d. She saw a search plane fly over.

6. What did Yuki remember that helped her find her way back to where she slept?
   a. She remembered she napped under a tall, bald pine tree.
   b. She remembered what the trail back to her sleeping spot looked like.
   c. She remembered a steep cliff by her sleeping spot.
   d. She remembered a waterfall splashing next to her sleeping spot.

7. How did Yuki know the explorers hadn't come back looking for her yet?
   a. They weren't waiting for her at her sleeping spot.
   b. They hadn't left a note for her to find at her sleeping spot.
   c. Their footprints were all going one way toward the Blue Hole.
   d. She didn't hear any voices yelling her name.

B A **simile** is a comparison of two things using *like* or *as*. A **metaphor** is a comparison of two things that are not very similar. The words *like* or *as* are not used. Read the sentences below. Write an **M** next to each metaphor and an **S** next to each simile.

M 1. Fingers of light slanted sideways through the trees.

S 2. Yuki had a vicious thirst.

S 3. Her face felt like a raging fire.

M 4. Yuki's tears made the forest dip and shimmer, turning it into a watercolor.

M 5. Yuki's mouth felt dry and furry like a small animal.

S 6. She ran through the forest like a wild deer.

M 7. The bees buzzed, the birds sang, and the squirrels chattered. The forest symphony began again.

S 8. The bald tree looked like an old, gnarled man.

S 9. Rocks were scattered around the forest like a giant's toys.

S 10. The footprints were arrows pointing the way.

M 11. The sun closed like a weary eye and sank behind the hills.

C The writer in "Yuki Finds Her Way" uses descriptive action verbs. Next to each action verb listed, write a synonym for it. **Synonyms** are words that mean the same or almost the same.

1. quarreled ___ suggest

2. excited ___ happy

3. snubbed ___

4. struggled ___ hard time

5. scrunched ___ squezzed

6. clawed ___ scrached

7. vicious ___ ferouis

8. leaped ___ hop

D Details in a story tell **where, when, why, how, who,** and **what** about the topic and/or the action. Skim the story "Yuki Finds Her Way" to find these details or facts. Write the key words that help you locate the information and then answer the questions.

1. What kind of tree did Yuki rest under?

   _____pine_____

2. What kind of trail did Yuki lose her way down?

   _____deer trail_____

3. How full was Yuki's water bottle before she emptied it?

   _____half   full_____

4. What is the name of the Explorers Club leader?

   _____Ms. Reesves_____

5. What is the name of the friend Yuki quarreled with?

   _____Jada_____

6. Describe the strategy Yuki used to make her way back to her "sleeping tree."

   _____find   the   tree_____

   _____

   _____

   _____

who?   **when?**

what?   **where?**   **why?**   **how?**

38

Do You Have the Time?

Have you ever wondered how people told time before the invention of the wind-up clock or the digital watch? In ancient times, people used something called a sundial, or shadow clock, for keeping time. The first sundial was probably just a simple pole or stick in the ground. People looked at the direction and length of the shadow cast by the stick to determine the time of day.

You may have observed that at sunrise your shadow is very long. In fact, it's longer than you are. And, you may have seen that at sunset your shadow is long, too. But it points the other way. In the middle of the day, the Sun is highest in the sky. Then your shadow is very short. It looks like a small dark spot around your feet.

Think of yourself as the pin of a sundial. As the pin, you cast a shadow. The pin on a sundial works the same way. The pin sits in the middle of a flat plate, which is marked with hours of the day. The directions *North* and *South* are marked on the plate.

The pin's shadow changes throughout the day. The length of the shadow depends on the height and angle of the Sun. As the Sun moves across the sky, the pin's shadow falls on each hour of the day, showing the time.

By 2000 B.C., people in Egypt and China were making sundials that could be carried from place to place. More advanced forms of the sundial were developed by the Greeks and Romans around 600 B.C. They created bowl-shaped dials with hour lines marked in the hollow of the bowl. The Romans even made sundials that could be worn as rings or on wristbands. But there was a problem. There were no shadows on cloudy days, making it hard to tell the time from season to season.

You can make your own sundial with just a few simple materials. They include:

- a watch or clock
- glue
- a paper plate
- a long, sharpened pencil
- a ruler
- an empty thread spool
- a compass
- a marker

After you gather the necessary materials, you are ready to make a sundial. First, glue the spool to the middle of the paper plate. Then, stand the long, sharpened pencil in the hole of the spool, with the pencil's eraser on the bottom. This pencil is your pin. (Be careful when working with the sharpened pencil to avoid injuring your eyes or skin.) Next, use the marker to draw a mark anywhere on the edge of the plate. Label this mark with an *S* for south. This mark will be used to align your sundial with Earth's axis.

Find a window or a spot outdoors that is in full sunlight all day. Put the sundial in this sunny spot after sunrise. Then, use a compass to make sure the *S* label points south. This label keeps your sundial in the same relationship to the Earth and the Sun all day long. When your watch reaches the nearest hour, use the ruler to draw a straight line along the length of the shadow cast by the pin. Label the hour next to the line you drew. For example, when your watch reads 8 A.M., draw your line along the pin's shadow and label it 8 A.M. Hint: To make it easier to draw on, you may want to place the paper plate on a hard surface, like a clipboard.

Repeat this step every hour, keeping the *S* label pointing south. Check the time, draw along the pin's shadow, and label the line with the hour. The last line you draw on your sundial is the last hour before the Sun sets.

When you have a line for each hour of sunlight, your sundial is finished. You can put it anywhere in the Sun, making sure the *S* label always points south. The pin's shadow will point to the hour of the day.

You can make your sundial more permanent by using a cement stepping stone instead of a paper plate. Use your imagination! Decorate the lines on the dial with bits of tile or small stones. Paint the spool and pencil with an enamel paint to make them weatherproof. Follow the example of early Romans and use Roman numerals to mark the hours. Place your finished sundial in a garden spot and always know what time it is. Unless, of course, it rains.

How Would You Decorate Your Sundial?

Write a description of how you would decorate your sundial. Include in your description where you would place your sundial. Provide a drawing of your sundial to go along with the description.

A **Underline the correct answer to each question.**

1. How would you classify "Do You Have the Time?"
   a. as a descriptive story
   b. as an autobiography
   c. as a short report
   d. as a how-to paper

2. What is another name for a sundial?
   a. shadow clock
   b. pin clock
   c. ring clock
   d. wristwatch

3. In this paper, the writer uses words like *first*, *next*, and *then*. Why?
   a. The writer has no specific purpose for using these words.
   b. The writer uses these words to help the reader imagine the sundial.
   c. The writer uses these as a clue to the order of steps in the process.
   d. The writer wants to use metaphors and similes to liven up the paper.

4. Why must the label "S" on the sundial always point south?
   a. The label stands for "stick in one place."
   b. The label aligns the sundial consistently with Earth's axis.
   c. The sundial looks more attractive when it is pointed south.
   d. The label means "this side up."

5. How did the sundial change in Roman times?
   a. The Romans made sundials larger and out of precious metals.
   b. The Romans made sundials for chariots and horse bridles.
   c. The Romans made sundials that could be worn on necklaces.
   d. The Romans made sundials that could be worn as rings or on wristbands.

6. Why doesn't the sundial work in cloudy weather?
   a. The sundial is powered by solar energy.
   b. The clouds block the wind that turns the sundial.
   c. Clouds have moisture that clog the pin on the sundial.
   d. Clouds block the sun's light on cloudy days and prevent a shadow.

7. Why do you think the author of this paper lists the materials before telling the procedure for making a sundial?
   a. The author is a very organized person.
   b. It saves time to collect the materials before beginning a project.
   c. It is important to know if you can afford the materials before beginning.
   d. The author wants to get the materials straight in his mind.

Synonyms are words that mean the same or almost the same. Circle the two synonyms on each line.

1. permanent   (passing)   brief   lasting
2. recede   resume   (quit)   start again
3. (accidentally)   invite   intended   meant
4. kindness   vicious   mean   (upset)
5. (fought)   made up   survived   quarreled
6. (flexible)   fumbled   (acted clumsy)   discovered
7. searched   abandoned   (revealed)   left behind
8. happy   lighthearted   moody   (glum)
9. negative   affirming   (photographed)   positive
10. pretend   biography   (imaginary)   report
11. march   align   line up   (mess up)

Choose a word from the Word Box below to complete each sentence. Some words may not be used.

Word Box

digital	reassemble	weatherproof
outcropping	resume	snubbed
deliberately	canopy	parched
vicious	intended	desperately
undoubtedly	retrace	reactor

---

1. To put something back together is to _____ reassemble _____.

2. A group of rocks sticking out of soil is called an _____ outcropping _____.

3. To act in a very careful and thoughtful way is to act _____ undoubtedly _____

4. To paint something so that it is protected from the weather is to make it
   _____ weatherproof _____

5. The top of a forest is called the _____ canopy _____.

6. To only act in response to something is to be a _____ reactor _____.

7. To go back over your steps is to _____ retrace _____

8. A computer image is _____ digital _____.

9. To have been very thirsty is to have been _____ parched _____.

10. To act in a panicked way is to act _____ vicous _____

Read the article below and study the diagram.

A Food Web

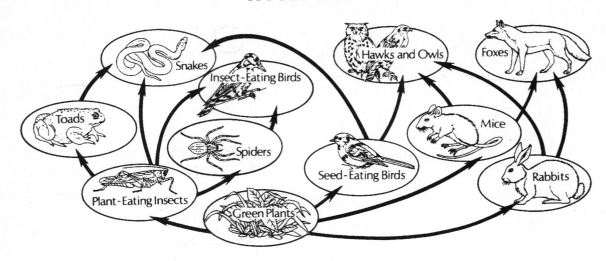

   All living things need energy to carry out necessary life processes. Organisms that get energy from sunlight through photosynthesis are called producers. All green plants, such as grasses and seaweeds, are producers.

   Organisms that eat each other are called consumers. Primary consumers like rabbits and insects eat producers to obtain energy. Secondary consumers like foxes and insect-eating birds eat primary consumers to obtain energy. Sometimes there are third-level consumers like owls and snakes that eat secondary consumers.

   A primary consumer is called an herbivore because it eats only berries, grasses, or other plant foods. Some secondary consumers are carnivores and eat only other animals. Other secondary consumers are omnivores and eat both plants and animals.

   The flow of energy among a group of plants and animals can be shown in a food web. A food web shows the energy relationships in an ecosystem. An ecosystem is a natural community of organisms and their surroundings. Ecosystems like deserts can be sparse, or bare, with few organisms. Ecosystems like forests can be rich, with many organisms.

Underline the correct answer to each question. Use the article and the diagram to help you.

1. Which sentence is a supporting detail from the first paragraph?
   a. All living things need energy to carry out necessary life processes.
   b. All green plants, such as grasses and seaweeds, are producers.

2. Which of the following is a conclusion supported by the details in the passage and the diagram?
   a. In a food web, energy flows from the Sun to producers and then to consumers.
   b. Consumers can obtain energy directly from sunlight or from producers.

3. What does a food web show?
   a. all the food that can be found in wilderness areas
   b. the energy relationships among animals in an ecosystem
   c. the energy relationships among organisms in an ecosystem
   d. the food that is no longer available to organisms in an ecosystem

4. Which one of the following is one of the consumers shown at the highest level in the food web?
   a. grasses
   b. rabbits
   c. mice
   d. owls

5. If all the grasses, berries, and trees in this food web disappeared, the immediate result would be that which of the following would have nothing to eat?
   a. owls
   b. foxes
   c. snakes
   d. rabbits

6. Which of the following is a supporting detail rather than a conclusion?
   a. Omnivores can be both primary and secondary consumers.
   b. Without energy from the Sun, no life on Earth would be possible.
   c. In ecosystems, an herbivore is always a primary consumer.
   d. Foxes get energy by eating mice and rabbits.

7. A hiker gets lost in the forest ecosystem. The food supply he brought with him runs out. As the hiker looks for food in the forest, what role is he likely to take on in the food web of the forest ecosystem?
   a. producer
   b. carnivore
   c. herbivore
   d. omnivore

8. According to the diagram, what level consumer is the spider?
   a. primary
   b. secondary
   c. third-level
   d. omnivore

The Mystery of the Missing Fossil

The day started foggy and rainy. Jeremy was stuck indoors with nothing to do. Or, at least nothing very interesting to do. His mother reminded him that he had a report that was due Monday morning.

Jeremy looked around his room for the fossil he was going to use as the basis for his paper. He had found the giant shell fossil the day before along the white rock banks of the creek that ran behind his house. He had looked up some interesting information on the Internet about the kind of fossil it might be. He had found some likely possibilities.

Jeremy scrabbled through the mess that was his room. An archeological dig might be necessary to find it if it was lost in his room. But the fossil was nowhere to be found.

Next he interviewed his younger sister, Jennifer. She admitted to having taken the fossil. "It was so pretty," she said sheepishly. "I put in on the desk in my room."

When they looked in Jennifer's room, only a bone was on her desk. Where had the fossil gone?

Cause and effect helps us understand plot. The plot must be understood in its proper sequence in order for it to make sense. It is similar to following the steps in a process in a how-to paper. Number the sections of this story to form a correct plot or sequence of events.

_____3_____ Jeremy took the fossil to his room, logged onto the Internet, and did a key word search on fossils. After looking at several sites, he found a web page that had pictures of a fossil shell similar to his.

_____5_____ Sunday morning dawned foggy and rainy. Jeremy was bored.

_____8_____ "Jennifer, did you take my fossil?" Jeremy yelled down the hall.

_____1_____ On Saturday, Jeremy explored the creek behind his house and found a huge shell fossil embedded in the limestone bank.

_____4_____ "This is great stuff," Jeremy thought to himself. "I'll bookmark this website and use it tomorrow to write that paper for science class."

_____6_____ "Why don't you get to work on your paper that's due Monday?" asked Jeremy's mom.

_____2_____ When Jeremy arrived home, he showed the fossil to his parents and his younger sister, Jennifer. "Can I have it?" she asked, looking at it with a gleam in her eye.

_____7_____ Jeremy grumbled a little and then started looking for his fossil so he could get to work on his paper. He looked all over his messy room, but the fossil was nowhere to be found.

_____9_____ Jennifer was in the living room. "Yes, it's so pretty. I put it on the desk in my room." But the fossil was not in Jennifer's room, either. They noticed a bone on the desk instead.

What happened to the fossil? Write your ending to the mystery on the lines below.

_____

_____

_____

_____

_____

_____

_____

_____

Skills Review (Stories 1–5)

 Read the article below. Note the details. Underline the main idea, or topic sentence, in each paragraph. Then answer the questions.

Captured Memories

1.   A unique way to capture your memories is with a time capsule. A time capsule is a box or container that has special items and papers placed in it that represent the time when the capsule is sealed and buried. The capsule is placed in a location that won't be tampered with. The time capsule is opened at a date years later.

2.   Select a box or container to hold the things that you will place in your time capsule. A large glass jar with a lid, a plastic box with a snap-on lid, or some other airtight container will be suitable. You can also decorate your container with images from the present.

3.   What do you put in your time capsule? Find things to put in your time capsule that you think represent your life now. You might think about including things that you know will change over time. Items might include a newspaper, pictures of people who are special in your life, a schedule from an important game, a list of your favorite music, and any other items that are important to you.

4.   You need to pick a safe and secret place to put your time capsule so that it won't be opened before you want it to be. You may want to talk to a parent about your time capsule and discuss possible places to hide it. After that, make a final decision about where you want to place your time capsule.

5.   When will the capsule be opened? You must decide on a date when you want the time capsule to be opened. The day might be some anniversary, like a birthday, graduation from college, or your marriage.

6.   You might want to create your time capsule with a friend or a group of friends. Make it a fun celebration. Share with each other when you plan to open the time capsule and then put it in the secure, secret location you have chosen.

1. What is the main idea of the fifth paragraph? Write the topic sentence.

   _____when____will____the____box__be__opened_____

   _____

2. Which paragraph makes suggestions about items to place in your time capsule?
   Underline the correct answer.

   a. paragraph 4   b. paragraph 5   c. paragraph 3

3. What is the main idea of paragraph 2? Underline the correct answer.

   a. Choose a secure, safe location for your time capsule.

   b. What is a time capsule?

   c. Select a box or container for your time capsule.

   d. Think about items you want to place in your time capsule.

4. What is paragraph 4 mainly about? Underline the correct answer.

   a. Find a glass jar with a tight-fitting lid.

   b. Include pictures, newspaper clippings, and a music list.

   c. Have a party with your friends.

   d. Pick a secure, safe location for your time capsule.

5. Which is the best title for the whole article? Remember that the title should tell
   what the article is mainly about. Underline the best title.

   a. A Snapshot of Your Life

   b. A Party Idea

   c. Bottle the Future

   d. Images: Past and Future

   e. Don't Dig Up the Past

6. Which step could you leave out and still succeed with your time capsule?
   Underline the correct answer.

   a. Have a party with friends.

   b. Find a safe location.

   c. Choose an air-tight container.

   d. Put items in the capsule.

   e. Tell at least one person where the capsule is and when you want
      it opened.

7. What would you put in your time capsule?

   _____under____a____volcano_____

   _____

   _____

   _____

Read the following article. Then follow the directions on the next page.

1.   Julie was hanging out at the park with her friends. She was running relay races with Jonika, who was also a good runner. Suddenly, Julie stumbled and fell down. Jonika hurried over to her. "What's up, Julie?" asked Jonika.

2.   "Not me," said Julie, holding back tears. "I just skinned my knee, and it really hurts. That soil in the track has washed out again. We just fixed that last week!" The park was in bad shape. The friends had talked often about the state of the park. "What are we going to do?" asked Jonika. "We don't have the tools we really need to fix the park. We need some help with these giant craters. It's like the surface of the moon around here."

3.   "What can we do?" asked Maria, thinking aloud. "Maybe we could write a letter to the editor of the local newspaper. If we could outline the problems in the paper, lots of people would take notice. Many people read and write letters to the editor."

4.   "Maybe we could make signs and protest," suggested Sam. "Then, everyone driving by would see us. Maybe they would stop and join in our cause. The local TV news will cover the story if enough people stop."

5.   "Before we do that, let's write a letter to the mayor," said Jonika. "Maybe he doesn't know how dangerous the park is. A younger kid might get hurt here easily. I read in the newspaper that a high percentage of children are injured on unsafe playgrounds."

6.   The group of friends put their heads together and wrote a letter listing all the problems with the park. A week and a half later, Mayor Carson made a date to meet the friends at the park. He met them at the gates with a repair crew. "I want to thank you all for alerting me to the danger here. There are so many parks and playgrounds in the city that it's hard to keep up with all that needs immediate attention."

7.   The friends met the following weekend at the park. They heard on the weather forecast that the weather was going to be sunny. The park looked beautiful and all of the tracks were in perfect condition. "Let's go for a run," Julie yelled at Jonika and Maria. Sam chimed in, "Wait for me!"

Draw lines to match each paragraph to its main idea.

Paragraph 1   a. The friends talk about making signs and protesting.

Paragraph 2   b. The friends talk about writing a letter to the editor.

Paragraph 3   c. The friends comment that the park is in bad condition.

Paragraph 4   d. The friends decide to write a letter to the mayor

Paragraph 5   e. The mayor brings a repair crew to the park.

Paragraph 6   f. The friends meet at the park to enjoy the repaired park.

Paragraph 7   g. One of the friends falls down.

What are some causes and effects in this story? Write them in the chart.

Cause	Effect
runing	skined knee
park is defecttive	writes letter park editor
letter to mayor	park fixed

Read the short biography and write a summary of it on the lines below.

Helen Keller and Anne Sullivan

As a baby, Helen Keller lost both her sight and her hearing. She also could not talk, so it was hard for her to let other people know what she wanted. In 1887 when Helen was almost seven, someone special arrived at her house. It was Anne Sullivan, a teacher of blind children. Helen seemed to dislike Anne from the moment she walked into the Keller home.

Anne Sullivan faced an incredible challenge. Not only did she have to win Helen's confidence and friendship, but she also had to teach someone who had no sense of language and no idea that objects have names. A breakthrough happened when Anne Sullivan poured water over Helen's hand and spelled the letters w-a-t-e-r on Helen's palm using sign language. Awareness suddenly came to Helen and she understood that the liquid she had in her hand had a name, *water*. As soon as she had this realization, she wanted to have the names of everything around her spelled into her hand. Anne had become Helen's "miracle worker." With Anne Sullivan's help, Helen learned to read.

Helen eventually went to Radcliffe College and Anne went with her. Helen Keller spent her life giving inspirational lectures and writing books on human rights issues. In 1964 she was awarded the Presidential Medal of Freedom. She was one of the first Americans to receive this medal for outstanding contributions to American life.

_____

_____

_____

_____

_____

_____

_____

_____

Circle two antonyms in each group of words below.

1. dull   moody   glossy   painted
2. despise   obvious   disable   hidden
3. panicked   elevated   friendly   snobbish
4. elevated   bored   eager   lengthen
5. happily   ferocious   glumly   disable
6. common   regulated   unique   discounted
7. expose   restrict   resign   free
8. reader   pored over   authored   scanned
9. canopy   range   roots   burn
10. elevate   provoke   condense   soothe
11. sit up   delay   recline   sleep

Circle two synonyms in each group of words below.

1. glumly   happily   sadly   upset
2. clattered   quietly   chattered   talked
3. reassemble   released   rebuild   detailed
4. scanned   chronicled   serious   reported
5. litter   landfill   trash   lighted
6. chaos   aching   uncaring   hurting
7. pick up   attachment   gather   assignment
8. emptiness   avoid   go around   meet
9. edit   weatherproof   command   protect
10. incredible   factual   fantastic   Martian
11. powered   scrunched   ate up   crumpled

F **Underline the correct answer to each question.**

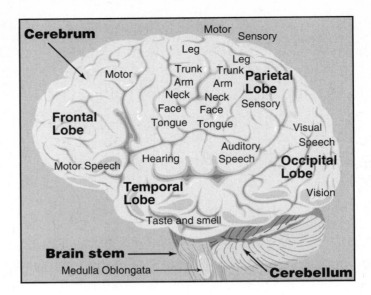

The human brain has three main parts: the cerebrum, the cerebellum, and the brain stem.

The cerebrum is the largest part of the brain. It is responsible for the senses, motor control, language, memory, and thought.

The cerebellum controls movements you make automatically, like standing up straight. It also coordinates information from the eyes, inner ears, and muscles to help maintain balance.

The brain stem controls heartbeat, breathing, and other vital functions of the body.

1. What would be the best title for this passage and diagram?
   a. The Human Nervous System   b. The Human Brain
   c. The Cerebrum   d. The Brain Stem

2. Which is the largest part of the brain?
   a. cerebrum   b. cerebellum
   c. brain stem   d. parietal lobe

3. According to the diagram, in which lobe is taste and smell located?
   a. frontal lobe   b. parietal lobe
   c. temporal lobe   d. occipital lobe

4. What part of the brain controls the heartbeat?
   a. cerebellum   b. cerebrum
   c. brain stem   d. frontal lobe

5. In what part of the brain is memory located?
   a. brain stem   b. occipital lobe
   c. cerebellum   d. cerebrum

Western or English?

Did you know that horses have been around since the time of dinosaurs? In fact, the horse is one of the oldest mammals in the world. Fifty million years ago, horses had four toes and were only eighteen inches high. That made them about as tall as a medium-size dog. Seven million years ago, horses had only one toe on each foot. They were also taller, about as big as modern-day horses. People tamed horses about nine thousand years ago and have been riding them ever since.

At first, learning to ride a horse was difficult. People were always falling off. Plus, they had nothing to protect their skin from rough horse hair. They didn't have shoes to protect their feet from the horse's sharp hooves, either. Over time, this changed. Nomads, or travelers, in ancient Asia invented stirrups, or footrests. These let riders stand up, turn, and duck down. Riders could also use them to make the horse jump and change direction.

Other inventions, such as saddles and horseshoes, let riders travel farther and do different kinds of work. The first horseshoes were actually shoes made from the hide of cows. The hide was tied onto the horse's hooves and left to dry. The Romans were the first to put metal shoes on horse's hooves.

Slowly, riding clothes, or apparel, changed, too. Pants made riding easier. Hard boots protected human feet from heavy horse hooves.

Today, there is a variety of clothing and tack, or equipment for riding horses. There are also two different styles of riding, called English and Western. Both styles have long histories. And both have their own clothing and tack, including saddles and reins.

English riding came to America from England in the 1600s. By the late 1700s, it was popular among wealthy Americans living in the eastern United States. These people thought the English way of riding was the proper way to ride. And riding became an important part of their social lives. People rode to visit friends, rode in hunting parties, and competed in horse shows.

The roots of Western riding can be traced back to the 1600s and 1700s. Cowboys called vaqueros worked on big Spanish ranches in the southwestern United States and northern Mexico. Western riding became more common in the middle and late 1800s. This was America's Wild West period. Cowboys and cowgirls worked hard and rode far in all kinds of weather. Many of them never left the saddle, doing all of their work from the back of a horse.

The ways riders sit and dress are different in English and Western riding. In English riding, the rider sits straight and tall in the saddle. He or she wears a black, flat-topped hat, a black long-tailed coat, white riding pants, and glossy black riding boots.

In Western riding, riders work with other animals, like cows or sheep. They must be able to move sideways, pull, chase, and do lots of messy work. As a result, their clothes are more practical. A rider wears a cowboy hat for shade. Blue jeans wear well through long hours of riding. Heavy, pointed boots protect toes and feet from the hooves of cattle or horses.

The English saddle was designed to be simple and light. The seat of the saddle is shaped to fit the horse and rider closely, so that they can move as one unit. Also, a light saddle means the horse has less weight to carry when it jumps.

The Western saddle has a horn in the front. This is a feature not found on English saddles. English riding requires lots of jumping. When a rider jumps, he or she must lean forward in the saddle. A saddle horn would get in the way. But cowboys and cowgirls use their horses and their saddles in other ways. The saddle horn gives a cowboy or cowgirl a strong object around which to tie a rope. Imagine a cowboy roping a steer. Once the rope slips over the steer's neck, the cowboy ties the end of the rope in his hand around the horn. This keeps the steer from slipping out of its noose or running away altogether.

The saddle horn is also handy when a cowboy or cowgirl needs to pull something, such as a fence post, using the horse's power. Horses used for Western riding are taught to walk backwards when they pull something so the rider can see what is happening. In Western riding, the horse and rider work as partners to get work done.

Western saddles are built with extra strong leather and stitching. This makes the saddle tough enough to stand up to hard use and bad weather. The seat of the Western saddle is designed for comfort, so the rider can work long hours in the saddle. Some cowboys and cowgirls slouch down and sleep on horseback if they have a long way to go, or if they have to stay with a cattle herd through the night.

Like the English saddle, English reins are designed to allow close communication between the horse and rider. Reins are part of the bridle, or harness attached to a horse's head. They allow a rider to use his or her hands to "talk to" or control the horse. There are two kinds of English bridles, a full bridle and a snaffle. A snaffle has a single bit, or metal part that goes in the horse's mouth. The snaffle bit is jointed in the middle so it "gives" when the rider pulls on the reins. The snaffle bit has one set of reins. A rider holds one rein in each hand. This makes it easy to control the horse when riding casually or in hunting parties.

The full bridle is more complicated. It has two bits that go in the horse's mouth, a snaffle bit and a curb bit. The curb bit is a straight piece of metal, and it exerts more pressure on the horse's mouth when the rider pulls the reins. The full bridle has two sets of reins, one for the snaffle bit and one for the curb bit. The rider must hold two reins in each hand, separated by the fingers. This allows the rider to have greater control over the horse. Control is especially important when a rider performs dressage. Dressage is a special kind of riding performed in horse shows. In dressage, a rider and horse move precisely. The rider sits very still while the horse performs intricate movements that look like equine ballet. The full bridle is also used in show jumping, when horses must jump over high fences, hedges, and water.

In Western riding, a rider holds both reins in one hand. Keeping one hand free is important. The free hand can hold a whip to urge a horse forward or rope an animal, such as a stray calf.

People and horses share a long, rich history that continues to be written today. Riding styles, clothing, and tack will continue to change, but the amazing human and horse partnership remains the same.

Which Style Would You Choose?

Have you ever ridden a horse? Would you like to? Write a short story about your day out riding, real or imagined. Include the style of riding you know or would like to learn in your description.

A **Underline the correct answer to each question.**

1. What is the best title for this story?
   a. Two Styles of Riding
   b. Learning About Horses
   c. Ancient Horses
   d. How to Take a Fall

2. What is the story comparing?
   a. riding in California and riding in Montana
   b. people who love horses and people who don't
   c. horses in the past and in the present
   d. Western and English riding styles

3. What invention helps riders stand up, turn, and duck down while riding?
   a. horseshoes
   b. reins
   c. bridles
   d. stirrups

4. Who first put metal shoes on horses?
   a. the Romans
   b. the Greeks
   c. the English
   d. the cowboys

5. What are cowboys on Spanish ranches called?
   a. rancheros
   b. vaqueros
   c. horse breakers
   d. cow punchers

6. The Western saddle has what in the front?
   a. a rope
   b. a horn
   c. a stirrup
   d. a trailer hitch

7. Why is the English saddle light?
   a. to make riding easier
   b. to help the rider rope a cow
   c. so the rider can lift it
   d. to make jumping easier

8. What is Western-style riding designed for?
   a. jumping
   b. visiting
   c. working
   d. hunting

59

B Summarize the story by making a chart. Use the charts below to list ways English and Western styles of riding are alike and different.

How English and Western Styles of Riding Are Alike

both   having   long story

own   clothing

How English and Western Styles of Riding Are Different

saddle   ho   horns   light
weight.

Use the information in the bar graph below to answer the questions.

United States Riders in Millions

Western-style Riders			
English-style Riders			

10   20   30

1. How many Western-style riders are there in the United States?
   a. 30 thousand
   b. 10 million
   c. 30 million
   d. 20 thousand

2. How many riders are there in the United States?
   a. 10 million
   b. 50 million
   c. 30 million
   d. 100 million

3. According to the bar graph, which statement below is true?
   a. Fewer women ride English-style than women ride Western-style.
   b. More men than women ride.
   c. More people ride Western-style than English-style.
   d. More people ride English-style than Western-style.

4. What percentage of males ride English-style?
   a. 20 percent
   b. 30 percent
   c. 10 percent
   d. not shown

5. Why do you think there are more Western-style riders than English-style?

   _____

   _____

   _____

   _____

D **Most poets make comparisons in their work. Often the comparisons are not stated as they would be in "ordinary talk." You have to stay with a poem to understand the comparisons and feel their power. Read the following poems. Then answer the questions below.**

Prancing

I dress up in black and white—
my boots are black as night and bright.
I hold myself erect and proper
I buckle my topper and off we go—
My ride and I, we move as one
leaping hedges at a flying run.
In show rings, we prance and trot,
Proud as any peacock, precise as any
clock; we canter, we gallop, we stop.

Working

My night-light is the evening star—
the cattle's lowing lulls me.
Through the wee hours I rock along
like a dozin' babe in a leather cradle.
Half in a dream, I keep watch,
with one eye and both ears open,
Alert to any danger, seen or herd.
As I ride the range I'm able
to protect the cows from corral to stable.

1. What is the poet comparing to a "leather cradle" in "Working"?

   Saddle

2. What is the poet comparing to being "proud as a peacock, precise as any clock" in "Prancing"?

   English Riding

3. What kind of work is the poet talking about in "Working"?

   Cattle drive

4. What homophone, or play on words, is the poet using in line 7 in "Working"?

   herd   heard

5. Why do you think the poet uses the words "'erect," "proper," and "topper," in "Prancing"?

   Englis Riding

E There are different ways you can compare one thing to another. Sometimes you can compare pairs of things to each other. This type of comparison is called an analogy. You need to think about how the first two things are related to each other. Then think how the next pair should be related to each other. Complete each analogy by circling the correct word.

Examples:

a. *Baseball* is to *bat* as *tennis ball* is to *racket*.
   (You use a bat to hit a baseball. You use a racket to hit a tennis ball.)

b. *Rider* is to *horse* as *biker* is to *bike*.
   (A rider rides a horse. A biker rides a bike.)

c. *Artist* is to *painting* as *musician* is to _____. (All the words are alike because they deal with artistic activities. Which word that expresses artistic activities would fit in the comparison and make sense?)

   gardening   (music)   training

1. Cowboy is to cattle as shepherd is to _____.
   (sheep)   chickens   horses

2. Hedge is to bush as forest is to _____.
   wilderness   desert   (tree)

3. Clean is to dirty as precise is to _____.
   exact   (sloppy)   snobbish

4. Leash is to dog as a bridle is to _____.
   cattle   horn   (horse)

5. Feathers are to birds as apparel is to _____.
   (people)   horses   fish

6. Tack is to riding as rope is to _____.
   (climbing)   swimming   snow skiing

7. Surgical tool is to medicine as computer is to _____.
   biology   geology   (technology)

8. Dozing is to sleeping as nibbling is to _____.
   (eating)   waking   drinking

9. Person is to house as horse is to _____.
   wagon   (stable)   guest house

F Find a word from the Word Box that is a synonym for the underlined word or words in each sentence. Then write each sentence using the new word.

┌─────────────── Word Box ───────────────┐
│ intricate   precise   hedge   │
│ nomads   apparel   tack   │
└───┘

1. The measurement was <u>exact</u> because all the numbers were carefully defined.

_____ *pressise* _____

2. The fashion model wore the latest <u>clothes</u>.

_____ *apareal* _____

3. After riding, she carefully put away all the riding <u>equipment</u>.

_____ *tack* _____

4. He had jumped his horse over the trimmed <u>shrubs</u>.

_____ *hedges* _____

5. Ancient <u>travelers</u> found ways to improve horseback riding.

_____ *nomad* _____

6. The well-trained horse made the <u>difficult</u> movements look easy.

_____ *intricate* _____

  G Write the words from the Word Box that mean the same or almost the same as **precise** on the lines below.

┌─────────────────── Word Box ───────────────────┐
│ exact   girlish   distinct   │
│ defined   accurate   unfailing   │
│ scissored   sloppy   measured   │
│ neat   mistaken   vague   │
│ abrupt   unvarying   strict   │
└──┘

1. _____ *exact* _____   2. _____ *defined* _____

3. _____ *defined* *neat* _____   4. _____ *accurate* _____

5. _____ *unvaring* _____   6. _____ *disintie* _____

7. _____ *measured* _____   8. _____ *strict* _____

64

Story 1: African-Americans seeking opportunity found it in the saddle of a horse. Of the fabled cowboys, roughly one-quarter were African American. Many were of mixed African-American and Native-American ancestry. Others were on close terms with Native Americans. Many found equality with whites in the rough and ready company of ranch life.

In 1870, Bill Pickett was born in Oklahoma, the son of black Cherokees. Pickett left school in the fifth grade and began to work as ranch hand.

Pickett invented the practice of "bulldogging," in which a cowboy stops a steer by leaping out of his horse's saddle onto the steer's back. Then, the cowboy grabs the steer's horns and twists until the steer's head is turned around. The steer then loses its balance and falls to the ground. Pickett always ended his act by sinking his teeth into the steer's upper lip in the manner of a bulldog, raising both hands to demonstrate that the animal was held down only by his strong teeth.

Pickett's unique skill earned him a job at the 101 Ranch in Oklahoma, a huge spread where cowboys were so talented at the rodeo that they were barred from local competitions. Zack Miller, one of the owners of the 101, organized a traveling rodeo show featuring the cowboys of the 101. Pickett's bulldogging took him to exhibition shows in Mexico, England, Argentina, and Canada— and in New York City's Madison Square Garden.

Story 2: Calvin Wilson left the plantation where he'd been a slave and set out for the Wild West in 1866. His reputation as a cowboy spread quickly. People told in amazement about how Cal could tame a herd of buffalo by just talking to them. They told how he could talk to hawks and rattlesnakes, too.

One day, Cal was showing off to a group of cowboys in Montana. He spun his lasso around his head until the loop was as big as a swimming hole. A group of wild mustang horses came thundering up just then and Cal spun the huge loop at them. He caught 25 mustangs in that one valiant throw. Another time Cal caught a grizzly bear with one hand and tamed it by tickling it.

Cal Wilson did many other amazing things that no one ever recorded.

Underline the correct answer to each question.

1. What is the best title for the first story?
    a. Rodeo Cowboys
    b. The 101 Ranch
    c. Bulldogging Bill Pickett
    d. Cowboys in Oklahoma

2. What is the story made up of?
    a. opinions
    b. facts
    c. metaphors
    d. similes

3. What kind of riding style did Bill Pickett most likely use?
    a. English
    b. dressage
    c. Western
    d. hedge jumping

4. What kind of story is the second story?
    a. a true story
    b. a persuasive paper
    c. a tall tale
    d. a short report

5. What word would you use to describe the second story?
    a. factual
    b. exaggerated
    c. newsworthy
    d. lengthy

6. What might be a good title for the second story?
    a. A Grizzly Attacks
    b. Calvin, A Regular Cowboy
    c. Calvin in Montana
    d. Cowboy Cal and His Magic Lasso

7. Where and when do you think the second story was probably first told?
    a. in a newspaper
    b. around a campfire
    c. at a business meeting
    d. in a political magazine

History Unraveled

Once a plant or animal dies, it begins to decay, or break down. That's how a body ends up as a skeleton. This process happens naturally unless nature or people interfere. Then the dead body is preserved.

A preserved body has been treated so that it does not break down. Unlike a skeleton, a preserved body keeps some of the soft materials it had while the person was alive. These materials include skin, muscles, and organs. In nature, bacteria and fungi help break down a body. They need oxygen and water to do their work. In some places, oxygen is missing. Bogs, or land that is soft and wet, are an example. In other places, water is frozen. Glaciers are an example. If oxygen is missing or if water is frozen, bodies don't break down. They can look as they did when the people died. That's why even today, people find bodies in bogs.

Bogs can preserve bodies so well that bodies thousands of years old can have skin, eyes, and hair. Scientists study the bodies they find in bogs to learn how people lived. Bodies may have food in their intestines, called entrails by ancient people, that tell scientists what these people ate. They may wear clothing that gives information, such as what the weather was like where these people lived. Bodies also tell secrets. They tell scientists why people died. Scientists look for signs of disease, accidents, and crime. There may also be objects buried nearby, such as jewelry and weapons. These objects tell scientists even more about people who lived long ago.

Ice preserves bodies, too. In 1991, hikers found a body in the Alps. Near the body, police and scientists found several tools, including an axe, a bow and arrows, and a small knife. The body wore a cape made from grass. It also wore a bearskin cap and leather shoes lined with grass. Scientists who studied the body determined that "Ötzi, the Ice Man" had lived about 5,000 years ago. He probably herded animals in the mountains.

People also prevent bodies from decaying. People in ancient Egypt, for example, believed that after death, a person moved to another world. They also believed the person needed the physical body that was left behind. Therefore, it was important to keep the body in good condition. So the Egyptians embalmed the body, or treated it with chemicals to preserve it. These preserved bodies are called mummies.

While the Ice Man was herding animals in the Alps, Egyptians were preserving their dead. The process, called mummification, took about seventy days. First, the embalmer, a special priest, removed all of the body's organs except the heart. Egyptians believed the heart was the center of a person's being. They also thought a person's intelligence lived in the heart. The organs removed from the body were preserved, too, and placed in special boxes and jars. Later in Egyptian history, embalmers would embalm the organs and then put them back into the body.

The body then had to be dried. Priests covered the body with natron, a natural salt. They also stuffed packets of natron inside the body. When the body was dry, the packets were removed and the body was rinsed. By this time, the body was shrunken and very dry, but still obviously human. Sometimes strips of cloth called linen were used to fill in spaces on the body. The body might also be given false eyes.

The next step in making a mummy was adding the linen cloth. Priests wrapped and enfolded the body with yards and yards of linen. Sometimes each finger and toe was wrapped separately before it was wrapped again as part of a hand or foot. Between layers of cloth, the priests coated the body with warm resin that gave the finished mummy a hard, smooth finish.

The mummification process was expensive. Few common people could afford it. As a result, members of the royal family were mummified most often. Using today's technology, scientists can learn much about Egyptian history by studying mummies. X-rays, for example, let scientists see inside the mummy without removing the wrappings. They can study small bits of bone to learn how tall people were and how long they lived. They can study unwrapped skin, fingernails, and hair to learn about the diseases Egyptians suffered and the medicines they took. And DNA samples let scientists make connections among branches of royal family trees.

The Egyptians aren't the only people to preserve their dead. Mummies have been found around the world, including in Asia, South America, North America, and Greenland. People in ancient Peru, for example, salted their dead. They wrapped their mummies in reed mats and then buried them under the floors of their houses. In Papua, New Guinea, the dead were smoke-cured and covered in clay. Then they were propped up so that they overlooked their villages. One of the most well-preserved mummies was found in China. The mummy, an embalmed woman who was an important person in the Han Dynasty, still has her skin, hair, fingernails, and even eyeballs.

Mummies teach us many things. They teach us about daily life and beliefs among people who lived thousands of years before us. They teach us about disease and medicine. They also teach us about the processes of preserving the dead. Whether created through natural or human means, preserved bodies are a link to the past.

What Kind of Dig Would You Go On?

Have you ever thought about being an archaeologist? What culture or period would you like to study? Write a description of a dig that you would like to be a part of. Include some of the scientific information in the story in your description.

A **Underline the correct answer for each question.**

1. Why do bogs prevent decay after death?
   a. The bog has a high level of salt in it.
   b. The mud has a natural moisturizer in it.
   c. Bacteria and fungi that break down a body can't live in a bog.
   d. Bog plants give off chemicals that help preserve the bodies.

2. Why is the Ice Man unusual?
   a. He was found with two other preserved people.
   b. He still had his tools and clothes with him.
   c. He was found with a book with his name in it.
   d. He was found in a hut that was covered with snow.

3. Why do scientists study preserved bodies?
   a. to satisfy their curiosity
   b. to identify the bodies
   c. to learn about bogs
   d. to learn how people lived

4. How did the Egyptians preserve bodies?
   a. They used X-rays.
   b. They embalmed them.
   c. They placed them in glaciers.
   d. They buried them in a bog.

5. What where Egyptian mummies wrapped in?
   a. grass
   b. clay
   c. reeds
   d. linen

6. What did Egyptian priests coat a body with to give it a hard, smooth finish?
   a. resin
   b. natron
   c. linen
   d. bog mud

7. How have scientists discovered connections between royal Egyptian families?
   a. by studying tools left in tombs by embalming priests
   b. by studying the clothes the mummies wore
   c. by studying DNA samples from mummies
   d. by studying jewelry and weapons

8. Where did people in ancient Peru bury their dead?
   a. under the floors of their houses
   b. in wells next to their houses
   c. on top of their houses
   d. in stables behind their houses

Egyptian Culture

The Egyptians built temples and statues of their gods. This shows the importance of religion in Egyptian culture. Egyptian people believed they passed into an afterlife when they died. Some of their most famous works of art were pyramids, tombs, and decorations in tombs.

Pyramids were huge tombs built for kings. A tomb is a place where someone is buried. The remains of some ancient Egyptian tombs, temples, and cities still stand today.

Egyptians believed that they needed to be buried with things they could use in the afterlife. Rich people built large tombs to hold these items. Kings were buried with jewelry, furniture, clothing, tools, and weapons. Many kings were buried with full-sized boats.

Some of the most exciting archaeological finds are tombs. Sometimes tomb walls have panels that have stories written on them in hieroglyphics. Archaeologists study the hieroglyphics to find out about the person buried there. Some tell stories about the afterlife.

Paintings cover the walls of tombs, too. Scientists study the paintings to learn about Egyptian beliefs. Much of the art in tombs shows what daily life was like in ancient Egypt. Some of the tomb paintings show farmers gathering barley. Others show servants bringing food or fanning their masters. Still other paintings show families eating or sitting together. They also show children playing games, adults watching plays, or people dancing.

Most tombs were robbed of their riches over the years. But archaeologists found the unopened tomb of King Tutankhamen, known as Tut. King Tut was a king who died very young. The unopened tomb helped archaeologists learn how Egyptian kings were buried. The organs of the king were found preserved near the body and placed in special boxes and jars. The king's heart was left untouched.

Imagine that you have been assigned a paper about Egyptian mummies and culture. On the lines below, create an outline to organize your thoughts. Use "History Unraveled" and "Egyptian Culture" to create your outline.

Egyptian Mummies and Culture

_____

_____

_____

_____

_____

_____

_____

_____

_____

_____

_____

_____

_____

_____

Choose words from the Word Box to solve the crossword puzzle.

Word Box

natron	pyramid	sick
enfold	linen	organs
adults	afterlife	resin
riddle	mummified	priest
mummy	enter	Alps
embalm	steam	panels

Across

1. An Egyptian tomb is found here
3. To preserve a body with chemicals
4. Hot, moist air
6. A preserved Egyptian body
8. A fabric used in embalming
10. This salt is used to preserve bodies
11. The opposite of <u>healthy</u>

Down

2. Another word for <u>grown-ups</u>
5. Egyptian priests did this to dead bodies
7. Sections of walls in tombs
9. The opposite of <u>exit</u>

Write a word from the Word Box to complete each sentence.

┌─────────────────── **Word Box** ───────────────────┐

embalm	mummies	resin
process	interfere	preserved
glaciers	intestines	bacteria

└──┘

1. Egyptian bodies wrapped in linen are called _____.

2. Egyptian priests used chemicals to _____.

3. Huge areas of ice that move as a sheet are _____.

4. Some microscopic organisms are called _____.

5. An action that takes more than one step is a _____.

6. To hinder something from happening is to _____.

7. The organs in the lower abdomen are called _____.

8. To have kept something from decaying is to have _____ it.

The International Space Station

The International Space Station (ISS) is the combined work of women and men from sixteen countries. They have come together to place a special community of scientists in orbit 250 miles above Earth. The participating countries are the United States, Russia, Canada, Japan, Brazil, and the European Space Agency (Belgium, Britain, Denmark, France, Germany, Italy, the Netherlands, Norway, Spain, Sweden, and Switzerland). These countries are spending billions of dollars, working for years, and facing the dangers of space to build the space station. Why? Because they believe the benefits of the space station will outweigh the huge costs.

The ISS is like a giant puzzle that is being put together high above Earth. The first piece of this puzzle is a Russian module, or section, called *Zarya*. *Zarya* was delivered into orbit November 20, 1998. Two weeks later, on December 4, 1998, the United States module *Unity* was launched into space. On December 7, 1998, *Zarya* and *Unity* were joined. More than 100 pieces must be built and shipped to Russia or the United States. Then, these pieces must be launched into space and joined before the station is complete. Building is expected to continue until April 2006.

Building a space station that is more than 600 feet long and weighs more than one million pounds is a big job. All together, there will be 46 launches. They include 37 U.S. space shuttle launches and nine Russian launches. When they arrive at the orbiting building site, astronaut teams will make at least 160 space walks to put the pieces together. They do this, of course, while the space station is moving at 17,500 miles per hour. That means that the station orbits Earth once every 90 minutes.

On their way to the ISS, astronauts wear special space suits. Inside the space station, astronauts wear regular clothing. But they must wear pressurized space suits during space walks.

These suits are able to withstand flying debris. They also protect the astronauts from dramatic temperature changes. Temperatures outside the station can range from 120 degrees below Fahrenheit in the station's shadow to 250 degrees in the sun.

When the ISS is finished, people from around the world will live and work there for long periods of time. Scientists will study the effects of zero gravity on plants, animals, chemical processes, and humans.

Zero gravity causes human bones and muscles to become weaker. This weakness can be seen in astronauts who return from long stays in space. They are sometimes unable to walk without help. If humans are going to live in space, scientists need to know more about the effects of zero gravity on the human body. The ISS will let scientists study these effects and develop solutions for problems that come with spending a lot of time in space.

Zero gravity also causes changes in chemical processes. This means that new drugs and materials can be created and tested only in space. The cure for the common cold, for example, might be found in space. Scientists aboard the ISS may create new combinations of metals for building homes on Earth.

Living and working in space will certainly be different from life on Earth. But the ISS has been designed for comfort. It is divided into living areas that are roomy and bright. Temperatures are kept at a constant 70 degrees Fahrenheit. Comfort is important because astronauts will be busy. In a typical workday, they will spend 14 hours working and exercising, 1.5 hours preparing and eating meals, and 8.5 hours sleeping.

Because of zero gravity, exercise is even more important on the ISS than it is on Earth. To fight the loss of muscles and bones, astronauts on the station must exercise. They will use bikes, rowing machines, and other equipment for about two hours every day.

For meals, astronauts will have a galley, or special dining room. In early space missions, astronauts ate meats and vegetables that looked like baby food. Today, space food looks like food we enjoy on Earth. Plus, the ISS has water, microwave ovens, and refrigerators. This lets astronauts eat more familiar types of food, including fruit, vegetables, and even ice cream!

Each astronaut will have a private room, or berth. With no gravity, there is no need for a regular bed. A sleeping bag keeps each astronaut from floating away. That might sound like a strange way to sleep, but astronauts from past space missions say that they enjoy sleeping in space.

Zero gravity makes simple tasks like brushing teeth a lot harder. Water doesn't flow in a stream. It forms bubbles. Astronauts will use a closed shower and vacuum to catch the bath water. To go to the bathroom in space, astronauts will use a special air toilet that uses flowing air instead of water to get rid of waste.

The International Space Station will become a new moon above Earth, seen even during the day. A glance upward at the sky will be a reminder of the fact that humans have finally built a home away from home. The ISS will also be a reminder of the creative work that people from different countries can do when they work together.

What happens next?

What other new things do you think might be discovered in space? Write a short paragraph about a discovery or invention that might come from space exploration. Include some of the scientific information from the story in your paragraph.

A **Underline the correct answer for each question.**

1. What is this article most like?

   a. a movie review

   b. a factual report

   c. a science fiction story

   d. a how-to paper

2. How many countries are working together on the ISS?

   a. fifteen

   b. thirteen

   c. sixteen

   d. fourteen

3. What was the first module of the space station to be put into orbit?

   a. the Russian module *Ursa*

   b. the United States module *Challenger*

   c. the United States module *Unity*

   d. the Russian module *Zarya*

4. How many pieces or modules must be launched to complete the ISS?

   a. more than 100   b. 150

   c. around 50   d. more than 200

5. How many total launches will be required to complete the ISS?

   a. 57   b. 37

   c. 46   d. 9

6. How often does the space station orbit Earth?

   a. every 60 minutes

   b. every 90 minutes

   c. every 120 minutes

   d. every 3 days

7. When astronauts are outside the space station, what must they wear?

   a. regular clothing   b. dress suits

   c. titanium suits   d. pressurized suits

8. What will scientists study the effects of?

   a. microwave ovens

   b. private berths

   c. zero gravity

   d. flying debris

78

Planet in Order from the Sun	Number of Moons	Order by Size	Description
Mercury	0	8	Hot planet; the surface is similar to Earth's moon.
Venus	0	6	Hotter than Mercury; carbon dioxide atmosphere; Venus has no life.
Earth	1	5	Earth has a core of iron; semi-fluid mantle; plates on mantle.
Mars	2	7	Mars is a red planet; has the largest mountain in the solar system.
Jupiter	several	1	Jupiter is mostly made up of gases and has rings.
Saturn	several	2	Saturn is made up of gases and has a rock core; rings made up of tiny particles.
Uranus	several	3	Uranus is mostly made of rocks, ice, gases; blue in color, thin rings.
Neptune	8	4	Neptune is blue in color, thin icy rings.
Pluto	1	9	Pluto is a cold planet far from the Sun.

Underline the correct answer for each question.

1. What two planets are closest to the Sun?
   a. Jupiter and Saturn
   b. Pluto and Neptune
   c. Mercury and Venus
   d. Earth and Mars

2. What do Jupiter, Saturn, Uranus, and Neptune have in common?
   a. craters
   b. high mountains
   c. hot atmosphere
   d. rings

3. Which planet is red?
   a. Mars
   b. Earth
   c. Neptune
   d. Saturn

4. Which is the largest planet?
   a. Earth   b. Jupiter
   c. Saturn   d. Pluto

5. What is the smallest planet?
   a. Neptune   b. Pluto
   c. Mercury   d. Venus

6. How many moons does Neptune have?
   a. 1
   b. several
   c. 2
   d. 8

7. Mercury's surface is similar to what planet's moon?
   a. Pluto's   b. Mars'
   c. Earth's   d. Neptune's

8. Which planet has a semi-fluid mantle with plates?
   a. Mars
   b. Earth
   c. Venus
   d. Saturn

C Write a summary on the lines below of the short report called "The International Space Station." Remember, a summary is a brief restatement of the main points of a paragraph or article.

_____

_____

_____

_____

_____

_____

_____

_____

_____

_____

_____

_____

_____

_____

_____

_____

D Choose a word from the Word Box to complete each sentence. Some words may not be used.

┌─────────────────────── **Word Box** ───────────────────────┐

debris	participating	galley
launched	withstand	pressurized
reminder	shuttle	dramatic
international	combination	missions
berth	astronauts	zero gravity

└──┘

1. To have sent something into space is to have _____ it.

2. A person who is joining in is _____.

3. Litter is sometimes called _____.

4. A vehicle that takes people or things from one place to another is a

   _____.

5. Space suits must be _____.

6. To be weightless is to have _____.

7. To hold up under stress is to _____.

8. If something is extreme it is _____.

9. The dining room in a ship is called the _____.

10. A sleeping compartment in a ship is called a _____.

E From the article called "The International Space Station," list four effects of the Space Station. Use a word from the Word Box above in each of your four answers.

_____

_____

_____

_____

_____

_____

_____

A hypothesis is a guess that is made to explain a certain event or fact until the actual cause can be proved. Read each of the following paragraphs. Write a hypothesis to explain what you think is happening in each paragraph. Then, write what you would do to prove your hypothesis.

1. You walk outside on a hot day. You notice that the border plants along the concrete walk are wilting and drooping.

Hypothesis: _____

_____

What could you do to prove your hypothesis? _____

_____

2. It's a cold day and the air is crisp and cool. You walk across a carpet and see that a piece of paper has stuck tightly to your pants leg. When you get to the door and touch the doorknob, you get an electric shock and the paper falls off your clothes.

Hypothesis: _____

_____

What could you do to prove your hypothesis? _____

_____

3. You are standing on a bridge and see a leaf floating along the smooth surface of a pond. Another leaf comes along and sinks when you disturb the surface of the water.

Hypothesis: _____

_____

What could you do to prove your hypothesis? _____

_____

4. Your dog starts to act nervous. You try to comfort her, but she goes into the other room and hides under the bed, shivering. You look outside and notice the wind is beginning to blow and the clouds darken.

Hypothesis: _____

_____

What could you do to prove your hypothesis? _____

_____

121 Earhart Lane
Los Angeles, California 90035

November 12, 2003

Station Manager
Space Age Channel Television Studio
P.O. Box 122
Washington, D.C. 20003

Dear Station Manager:

I am a big fan of your station. I think your educational programs about air and space are great. From one show, I learned that the first person to fly faster than the speed of sound was Chuck Yaeger. In another show, I learned that Neil Armstrong and Buzz Aldrin were the first people to walk on the moon. Now I watch your channel to learn about the International Space Station because I want to work there one day. Your channel has taught me a lot about the history of air and space travel. Even so, one important subject is missing. That subject is women. I've never seen a single program that describes the accomplishments of women in air and space.

Women have played important roles in powered flight since the early 1900s. Let me give you just a few examples. Bessica Raiche helped build the airplane she flew in 1910. Her first flight lasted only a few minutes, but she tried several more flights. Some call Raiche the "First Woman Aviator in America." In 1911, Harriet Quimby became the first American woman to earn a pilot's license. She was also the first woman to fly across the English Channel. In 1913, Katherine Stinson and her mother started a flying business.

Two years later, Marjorie Stinson joined the company. She started a flight school to train WWI pilots from the U.S. and Canada. In 1921, Bessie Coleman became the first African-American person to earn a pilot's license. She earned her license in France and then came back to the U.S. to raise money to build a flight school for other African-Americans.

I've given you only a few examples of the women who were part of America's air history. There are more. And the number grows even larger every year. By 1958, when NASA was formed, women were part of that, too. In fact, NASA's very first Chief Astronomer was Dr. Nancy Roman. Margaret W. Brennecke was a welder. She chose the metals and techniques for building the Saturn rockets that flew in the 1960s. She did the same for Spacelab and the Space Shuttle's rocket boosters. Many other women worked with the space program as engineers and scientists. In 1978, six women, including Dr. Sally Ride, joined NASA as astronauts. Twenty years later, Lt. Col. Eileen Collins became NASA's first female commander.

I've left out so many women. And so have you. Unless you include women, you're telling only half of the history of air and space travel.

Besides telling only half a story, you're missing the chance to send an important message to young girls and boys in school. Those children will probably grow up to live in space! This is a good time to tell all of them about how they can be a part of the future.

If you don't think preparing children for the future is your job, then you might think about the people who watch and support your channel now. My research tells me that more than half of the people who watch your channel are female. How long do you think they'll watch if you don't tell stories that include them? What will happen to your station when half of your viewers stop watching?

In closing, I'm asking you to include women in your station's programming. Tell women's stories to give a more complete history of air and space travel. Tell women's stories to help prepare young girls and boys for their future. Finally, tell women's stories to keep your viewers and your station! Act now so that I can watch your channel tomorrow.

Sincerely yours,

Jen Rumi-Stevens

Jen Rumi-Stevens

Future Space Station Commander

What happens next?

Describe how you think the station manager will respond to Jen's letter. Include in your paragraph any other arguments you think she could have used to achieve her goal of more programming about women.

A **Underline the correct answer to each question.**

1. What is the object of Jen's letter?
    a. to compliment
    b. to persuade
    c. to complain
    d. to inform

2. What is the one important subject Jen says is missing from the programming?
    a. men
    c. women
    b. outer space
    d. air travel

3. Who was the "First Woman Aviator in America"?
    a. Marjorie Stinson
    b. Amelia Earhart
    c. Harriet Quimby
    d. Bessica Raiche

4. Who was the first African-American woman to earn a pilot's license?
    a. Harriet Quimby
    b. Bessie Coleman
    c. Bessica Raiche
    d. Dr. Sally Ride

5. Why does Jen list so many examples of women in aviation history?
    a. The station has asked her for a list of aviators.
    b. She wants to let the station manager know what she has learned in school.
    c. She is giving support to her argument by listing examples.
    d. She wants the station to increase the number of aviators it talks about.

6. What is one of Jen's main points in support of her argument?
    a. The station is only telling half the story of air and space travel.
    b. The station's viewers are elderly and need more air time.
    c. The station is losing its male audience.
    d. The station is not appealing to the airline travelers in its audience.

7. What does Jen want the station to do?
    a. include more physically challenged people in the station's programming
    b. include more elderly in the station's programming
    c. include more women in the station's programming
    d. include more minorities in the station's programming

8. What support does Jen give for her request?
    a. research
    c. opinions
    b. feelings
    d. hopes

Read the article below about understanding Internet addresses.

If you open the mailbox and find a letter, the person who sent it wrote your name and address on the envelope. The address tells people at the post office where you live. If the address is correct, you receive the letter. But if something is missing or written incorrectly, you may never receive your mail. Finding a website is like sending a letter. You need an address, and you must write it correctly.

Parts of a Web Address, or URL

These letters tell your computer to go to a website. All URLs begin with these letters followed by a colon and two slashes.

Many URLs include www. That stands for World Wide Web.

http://www.NameOfWebsite.gov

These letters stand for another domain. This domain is the Top Level Domain, or TLD. It describes the kind of site you are visiting. Here, gov stands for government. In other words, the site is sponsored by the government. There are other kinds of TLDs, too.

These letters represent the domain. A domain is the name of the company or organization represented by a particular website.

A website's address is called the Uniform or Universal Resource Locator, or URL. All URLs begin the same way—http://. This group of letters and symbols is followed by more letters and symbols. Look at the diagram. It shows the different parts of a website address.

No two websites have exactly the same URL. Each URL is registered, or recorded, by an organization called the Internet Network Information Center, or InterNIC.

Thousands of URLs are registered every day. That's a lot of domain names. How can they all be different? Changing the TLD helps.

In the example URL http://www.NameOfWebsite.gov, the TLD .gov tells you that the website is a government site. The letters .com at the end of a URL tell you the website belongs to a business. If the address ends in .org, the website belongs to a research group or other organization. A fun and informative government site is www.cia.gov/cia/publications/factbook/index.html. There, you can learn and do research on different countries.

To meet the high demand for URLs, more domain names have been introduced. For example, you might see .info and .store at the end of a URL. Guess what these letters stand for. If you guessed information and store, you are right.

Domain names for websites outside the United States are different but simple to understand. Look at the last two letters in this URL: http://www.pm.gov.uk. The domain .uk stands for United Kingdom. Other country domains include .ca for Canada, .au for Australia, and .jp for Japan. You can travel around the world on the Web.

Doing research on the World Wide Web is a good way to supplement other kinds of research. There are many great informational websites about space and astronauts. Look at how the sample website is organized. (This is not a real website.)

Remember that information that is "hot" or "clickable" on a website is underlined. That means when you put your mouse over it, you will get a "pointy finger" cursor. When you click the hot link, you will be taken to another web page with information about that subject.

Answer the questions below about the information in the URL passage and information shown on the website example.

1. If a website is organized somewhat like an outline, what does the menu show?
   a. supporting details
   b. major topic headings
   c. title
   d. subheads

2. Who was the first woman spacecraft commander?
   a. Eileen Collins
   b. Ellen Ochoa
   c. Anna Low
   d. Mae Jemison

3. Who do you think was the first African-American woman in space?
   a. Ellen Ochoa
   b. Anna Low
   c. Mae Jemison
   d. Eileen Collins

4. What is the website's address or URL?
   a. www.spacenews.edu
   b. www.featuredwomen.com
   c. www.Flygirls.org
   d. www.womenaviationpioneers.com

5. What does an underlined word or name mean on a website?
   a. The word is the title of a book or movie.
   b. The word is underlined so that it will stand out.
   c. The word is "hot" and can be clicked to reach more information.
   d. The word is underlined for artistic effect.

6. What is a URL?
   a. a country abbreviation
   b. an abbreviation for the type of organization that sponsors the site
   c. a website address
   d. a domain name

7. What does "www" stand for in the URL?
   a. Who What Where
   b. We Want Websites
   c. Who Will Win
   d. World Wide Web

8. What does the TLD notation tell you at the end of a URL in the United States?
   a. the date the website was first posted
   b. how many people created the site
   c. what kind of organization sponsors the site
   d. what country the site originates from

9. What might the domain name represent on a commercial business site?
   a. the name of the sponsor
   b. the name of the business
   c. the name of the computer programmer
   d. the name of the owner of the business

10. What does "gov" at the end of a URL show?
    a. that it is a nonprofit educational site
    b. that it is a government-sponsored site
    c. that it is a business-sponsored site
    d. that it is a foreign site

11. Who keeps track of all the domain names so that there are no duplicates?
    a. Universal Resource Locator
    b. Top Level Domain
    c. Internet Network Information Center, or InterNIC
    d. World Wide Web

12. Where does the country abbreviation go on an international URL?
    a. at the end of the address
    b. in the middle of the address
    c. at the beginning of the address
    d. There is no country abbreviation.

The First Hispanic-American Woman in Space

When Ellen Ochoa became an astronaut in 1991, she became the first Hispanic-American woman in space. Since then, she has gone into space many times on the shuttle. In space, she has studied the effects of solar flare activity on Earth and Earth's atmosphere.

Ellen says life in space is very different from life on Earth. One very big difference is that there is no gravity there. Gravity is the force that pulls things toward the Earth. Gravity keeps us from flying off into space! So, in space, Ellen and the other astronauts have to learn how to float in zero gravity. In order to sleep, they tie their sleeping bags to a hook and float in their sleeping bags as they sleep.

Ellen Ochoa did not always want to be an astronaut. When she was a child, there were no women astronauts to follow. It did not seem like something girls did. Then, Ellen grew up and went to college and was exposed to women doing all kinds of interesting and valuable work. She did research in astrophysics and science at Stanford University.

Now, Ellen Ochoa has had an experience that not many people can claim. She has seen the earth from far away in space. She has trained hard with other astronauts to make sure that nothing goes wrong on their missions. Her greatest joy is flying into space to study Earth and the effects of space.

Underline the correct answer to each question.

1. When did Ellen Ochoa first become an astronaut?
   a. 1981   b. 2001   c. 1991   d. 1999

2. What has she studied in space?
   a. the effects of gravity on astronauts b. the effects of sun spots on Earth
   c. the effects of sleeping in space   d. the effects of going to college

3. How is life in space different from life on earth?
   a. There is only liquid food in space.
   b. There is no training in space.
   c. There is zero gravity in space.
   d. There is no sleep in space.

4. What is an example of gravity working?
   a. A paper airplane flies across the room.
   b. A helium balloon is released.
   c. An apple falls from a tree.
   d. A puddle of water freezes.

5. Why is it important to have good role models?
   a. They show us we should not look too high.
   b. They can inspire us to do amazing things.
   c. They show us we can do things without working hard.
   d. They can help us set our sights low.

Read the letter below and underline the main idea or topic sentence in each paragraph.

Springfield High School
1015 Second Avenue
Springfield, Texas 75909

January 6, 2004

Dr. J. Reese
Superintendent,
Springfield School District
1000 Main Street
Springfield, Texas 75909

Dear Dr. Reese:

Many parents, teachers, and kids believe that homework has gotten out of hand. Recently, our local newspaper printed an article by Janie McKee. She gave the results of a homework study done at the University of Texas. Did you know that today's primary school children do more homework than ever before? A first-grade student spends more than six hours each week doing homework. That's 44 more minutes of homework than students had in 1981. Even more surprising, older elementary students sit down to more than ten hours of homework a week. That's about three hours more than students had in1981. Plus, today's kids spend many hours a week doing other school activities, such as band, choir, sports, and drill team. All of these hours add up. Now you know why family time has almost disappeared.

I would like to suggest that our school district join the national movement called "Take a Night Off From School." Joining this program would give families at least one night to spend together. This would help free them from the stress of doing math problems, history reports, and other school projects.

Ms. McKee's article quoted Dr. Harris Miller, a professor at the University of Texas. It upsets kids and makes them feel bad about themselves when they don't have enough time to be part of important family activities. Dr. Miller points out that the National Parent-Teacher Association suggests a ten-minute homework rule. The rule says that kids should have ten minutes of homework times their grade level. For example, a first grader should have ten minutes of homework. As an eighth-grader, I should have no more than eighty minutes. That is one hour and twenty minutes of homework each night! Dr. Miller also points out that some students have less homework than this. Some students, like me, for example, have much more. My classmates and I believe this is a serious problem. So do our parents and many of our teachers. To sum up, in the words of Dr. Miller—too much homework has "negative results."

At this time, our district does not have rules regarding the amount of homework students should have each day. Without rules, teachers often assign only ten minutes of homework on Monday, but three hours on Thursday. This hurts not only students but parents as well. Family activities are hard to plan because the amount of homework on any night changes without warning. Homework limits would help solve this problem.

As a first step, I ask that you consider the "Take a Night Off From School" program. This national program encourages school districts to have one homework-free night each week. Recently, students, parents, and teachers in Sutton, New Jersey, had a successful homework-free night. There, school and community leaders worked together to pick a night for a "homework holiday." They chose a night with few or no scheduled community events. School and community leaders encouraged families to use the time to share dinner, visit a park, or play games together. The New Jersey "night off" was a big success. Now families have their community's support and encouragement to plan more family activities.

If you would like to know more about this successful national program, I would be happy to send more information. And, as a representative of the Student Council, let me assure you that our school and the P.T.A. would be happy to work with you. Plus, a representative of the "Take a Night Off From School" national organization has written to say she is willing to help our district. She will help plan and get community support for its first homework-free night. Working together, I know that we can begin to balance the needs of families with the need for a good education. I look forward to working with you.

Respectfully yours,

Chantal Warden

Chantal Warden
President
Springfield Student Council

B **Underline the correct answer to each question.**

1. What is the letter writer's main point?
   a. There is not enough homework being assigned.
   b. Too many outside activities take away from homework.
   c. Too much homework is being assigned.
   d. Teachers talk to one another too much about the homework load.

2. What program does she want the school district to join?
   a. Take a Night Off From Work
   b. Take a Night Off From Sports
   c. Take a Night Off From Family
   d. Take a Night Off From School

3. How does the letter writer back up her arguments?
   a. She mentions her own opinions and feelings.
   b. She quotes the opinions of parents.
   c. She lists the opinions of other students.
   d. She talks about the research and opinions of experts.

4. What does Chantal say the district does not currently have?
   a. a policy about after-school study rooms available to students
   b. rules concerning the amount of homework given to students
   c. a before-school tutor for students
   d. rules about dress and conduct for students

5. Who has already tried the national program Chantal is suggesting?
   a. Brooklyn, New York
   b. New Haven, Connecticut
   c. Taos, New Mexico
   d. Sutton, New Jersey

6. Who did Chantal say would help with this program?
   a. the football team and the cheerleaders
   b. the Spanish Club
   c. the Student Council, the P.T.A., and a program representative
   d. the Future Teacher's Association and the Latin Club

7. How does Chantal close her letter and help her case with the Superintendent?
   a. She ends it angrily.
   b. She ends it in a businesslike way.
   c. She ends it respectfully.
   d. She ends it abruptly.

8. What is the main reason Chantal wants to change the school district's policy?
   a. to give students more time for sports activities
   b. to give families more time together
   c. to give parents more time away from their children
   d. to give teachers more time to create lesson plans

Create an outline to show the organization of information that Chantal used in her letter to Dr. Reese. Remember, when you create an outline, follow these guidelines:

1. Use Roman numerals (I., II., III.) to list the main idea groups.
2. Use capital letters (A., B., C.) to list supporting ideas.
3. Use Arabic numerals (1., 2., 3.) to list details and examples.

D **Circle the correct analogy.**

1. <u>Parents</u> are to <u>chores</u> as <u>teachers</u> are to _____.

   homework   baby-sitting   parents

2. <u>President</u> is to <u>vice-president</u> as <u>superintendent</u> is to _____.

   janitor   teacher   principal

3. <u>Teachers</u> are to <u>students</u> as <u>parents</u> are to _____.

   pets   children   grandparents

4. <u>Musicians</u> are to <u>music</u> as <u>athletes</u> are to _____.

   baseball   sports   soccer

5. <u>Creative</u> is to <u>dull</u> as <u>positive</u> is to _____.

   negative   joyful   deep

E **Read this poem and answer the questions about poetic comparisons.**

> ### Homework
>
> I plow in as soon as I hit the door
> of home. Well, first I have to fuel up
> with snacks and drink.
> Then, I sink into a mountain of papers.
> Sometimes I wonder, are we all invisible vapors—
> ghosts, the teachers do not see?
> Perhaps they do not know how much they each
> have assigned us to complete?
> This feat, this mountain of papers,
> Will I reach the top?

1. Why does the poet use the word "plow"?

   _____

2. After having a snack, what is the poet comparing the load of homework to?

   _____

3. What is the poet comparing to "invisible vapors" or "ghosts"?

   _____

4. What is the "feat" the poet is probably talking about?

   _____

Choose a word from the Word Box to complete each sentence. Some words may not be used.

Word Box

regarding	accomplishments	national
primary	programming	international
impact	scheduled	possibility
lessen	aviator	negative
commander	superintendent	restrict

1. Good things that are achieved by people are called

_____.

2. A person who flies an aircraft is called an _____.

3. The person in charge of a crew on an aircraft is the _____.

4. The opposite of positive is _____.

5. To have marked something on a calendar is to have _____ it.

6. To hold something within limits is to _____.

7. To have an effect on something is to have an _____.

8. The leader of a school district is called the

_____.

9. One of many options is a _____.

10. Shows on television or the radio are called _____.

11. To decrease is to _____.

12. Something that involves many countries is called _____.

G **Use the bar graph to answer the questions.**

WORLD POPULATION GROWTH

In 1994 the world's population growth reached 5.6 billion people. By the year 2020, the population is expected to rise to 7.9 billion. Most of the population increase in the next 25 years will take place in the developing countries. In fact, of the 2.3 billion people added to the population, 9 out of 10 will be from developing nations.

1. By the year 2020, what is the world's population expected to increase to?
   a. 2.3 billion
   b. 5.6 billion
   c. 7.9 billion
   d. 13.5 billion

2. Which of the following is the main idea of the paragraph?
   a. Developing nations are growing rapidly.
   b. The world's population is increasing.
   c. World population growth is a problem.
   d. In 1994 the world's population was 5.6 billion people.

3. According to the bar graph, which statement below is true?
   a. World population was 300 million in the year 1 A.D.
   b. Population doubled between 1800 and 1900.
   c. In 1900 there were under one million people in the world.
   d. In 10,000 B.C. there were about 10,000 people in the world.

4. In 1700 how many million people were there in the world?
   a. 510
   b. 710
   c. 625
   d. 300

5. What do you think is meant by the phrase "developing nations"?
   a. established countries like the U.S.
   b. South American countries
   c. members of the United Nations
   d. countries that are poor and overpopulated

Solving the Garbage Problem

All across the United States, local governments are faced with the same growing problem—garbage. What is garbage? It's waste from our homes, businesses, schools, and hospitals. It's the stuff we don't need anymore. It's things we call useless. Americans produce nearly 210 million tons of solid waste each year! Then they demand that their cities find places to store it.

Finding cheap landfills, or places to put our mounting trash, is only part of the problem. People who work in landfills want more money. Plus, new laws add to the cost of storing garbage. These laws are meant to keep groundwater safe and reduce methane, the dangerous gas that comes from landfills. But they also mean we pay more to have our trash picked up and hidden.

People argue about how to solve the garbage problem. Some think we should build more and bigger landfills. Others think we should dump trash in the ocean. Still others say we should build expensive power plants that burn trash for energy. However, many experts think that the best long-term answer is something called the triangle of the three Rs. The three Rs stand for *Reduce, Reuse, Recycle*. Together, the experts say, these three Rs are the solution to our garbage problem.

Let's look at the first two Rs in the triangle—Reduce and Reuse. We often overlook ways to reduce and reuse solid waste. But if we are going to manage our trash, reducing and reusing are more important than recycling. We reduce our trash when we buy and use fewer things. That's because in time, the things themselves become trash. So does the material that was used to wrap them.

Consider ways you can reduce your trash. One way is to buy concentrated items. For example, when you buy orange juice, buy the concentrated kind. Concentrated juice is usually packaged in a small, paper container. You add water at home. The people who sell unconcentrated juice add water before they package the juice. You pay extra for the water and the larger, plastic container used to hold it.

Buying food or materials in bulk also cuts down on trash. This means that when you buy one huge bag of rice, for example, you make less trash than when you buy smaller bags.

Another way to reduce your trash is in your yard. There you can build a compost pile. Compost is a mix of food waste from your kitchen and cut grass and leaves from your yard. Stirring the compost helps it decay, or break down. Then you can add it to your yard or garden plants to help feed them and keep them moist. It also protects them from cold temperatures. Keeping a compost pile means usable plant waste stays at home instead of taking up space at a landfill.

Reusing is just as important as reducing the numbers of products we buy. Replace paper cups with china cups that can be used again and again. Carry cloth grocery bags to the grocery store. If you buy soda at the movies, pay attention to the specials. Some theaters sell plastic cups that you can use over and over again. And refills are cheaper.

Now let's look at the last R in the triangle—Recycling. Think for a moment about what you throw away in just one month. Chances are, if all of the trash you created were piled next to you, you would be standing next to a small mountain.

In 1988, the city of Phoenix paid for a garbage study. Leaders in the city wanted to know what people throw away. They hired Dr. Bill Rathje, of the University of Arizona Anthropology Department, to lead the study. Dr. Rathje and his team sorted and classified garbage from 500 homes. They learned that most of the garbage people threw away could be recycled. If we say that the trash in this study is like the trash we all throw away, almost 90 percent of the solid waste we create could be recycled. That means it never needs to reach the landfill!

Try as we might, we can throw out the garbage. We can carry it to the curb. We can even take it to the dump. But we can never really make our own mountains of garbage disappear. When we throw garbage away, it just goes somewhere else, and at a cost. Until we use the three Rs, we are stuck with our trash.

Many cities are so short of landfill space that they give recycling bins to homes and businesses to shrink the amount of solid garbage waste they pick up. When you do something as simple as recycling a soda can, you help reduce the amount of aluminum that is taken from the ground. You also help reduce energy use and the water and air pollution that come from processing the aluminum.

In many older landfills, toxic, or poisonous, substances leak into the groundwater that we drink or use on our crops. Cleaning up these leaks can be costly. Prevention makes more sense, and that's where recycling comes in. When you recycle motor oil, for example, you help keep toxic substances like lead out of your local landfill. That means you help keep them out of your air and water, too.

Of all the environmental problems we face, garbage is one problem you can really do something about. The choices you make every day affect the amount of garbage you throw away and the environmental problems you help create. When you follow the three Rs—Reduce, Reuse, Recycle— you lessen waste and the problems that go with it. You save natural resources, decrease the need for energy, and reduce air, water, and land pollution. You also save money.

Garbage isn't just your problem, but you are an important part of the solution. Following the three Rs saves money, benefits the environment, and protects your health. So start using the three Rs to manage your own mountain of garbage. Conquer your mountain with a cry of "Reduce, Reuse, Recycle" that can be heard around the world.

Any Ideas?

Tell about any ideas you have for reducing garbage and the problem of landfills. Describe what you and your family do to keep the planet clean.

A **Underline the correct answer to each question.**

1. How many tons of solid waste do Americans produce each year?
   a. 201 million tons   b. 300 million tons
   c. 210 million tons   d. 500 million tons

2. What adds to the cost of landfills?
   a. the type of garbage thrown away
   b. higher pay for landfill workers and new environmental laws
   c. special exhaust systems for the garbage trucks used
   d. the kind of dirt that is taken out of the landfill

3. What kind of dangerous gas can come out of landfills?
   a. helium   b. crude oil
   c. gasoline   d. methane

4. According to this article, what are some other ways people want to get rid of trash?
   a. dump it in the ocean or burn it in power plants
   b. bury it in their back yards
   c. send it on a ship to poorer countries
   d. put in inside of an extinct volcano

5. What is the triangle of the three Rs?
   a. Refuse, Renew, Redo
   b. Resell, Repel, Remake
   c. Reduce, Reuse, Recycle
   d. Resist, Reject, React

6. How can we reduce our trash?
   a. buy and use fewer things
   b. put our trash in our neighbor's bin
   c. eat less and make our parents eat more
   d. put the trash out less often

7. What is mixed with food waste to create compost?
   a. plastic wrappers
   b. cut grass from the lawn
   c. wooden posts
   d. glass bottles and caps

8. How much solid waste did the trash study report Americans could recycle?
   a. 50 percent of solid waste
   b. 90 percent of solid waste
   c. 60 percent of solid waste
   d. 100 percent of solid waste

B **Refer to the bar graph to answer the questions below.**

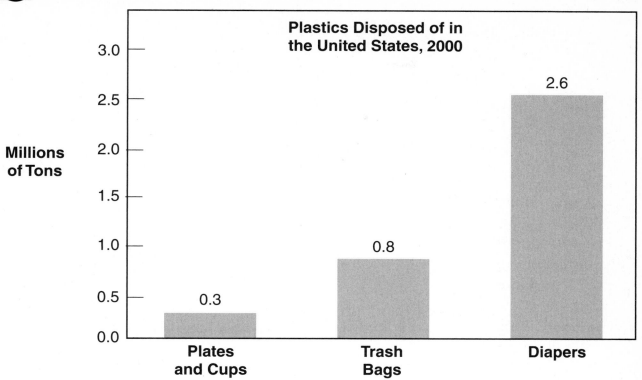

Plastics Disposed of in the United States, 2000

Millions of Tons

1. In 2000, Americans threw out how many tons of diapers?
   a. 0.3 million   b. 0.8 million
   c. 1.5 million   d. 2.6 million

2. Based on the information in the graph, what can you conclude?

   a. People in the United States have too many children.
   b. People in the United States do not waste anything.
   c. People in the United States do not use anything made of plastic.
   d. People in the United States buy a lot of disposable items.

3. Which of the following would be another good title for the graph?
   a. How to Recycle Plastics
   b. A Throwaway Society
   c. Plastics for Serving Food
   d. Too Many Diapers

4. According to graph, how many tons of plates and cups and trash bags were thrown out?
   a. 11.1 million   b. 1.1 million
   c. 0.5 million   d. 0.8 million

Refer to the circle graphs to answer the questions below.

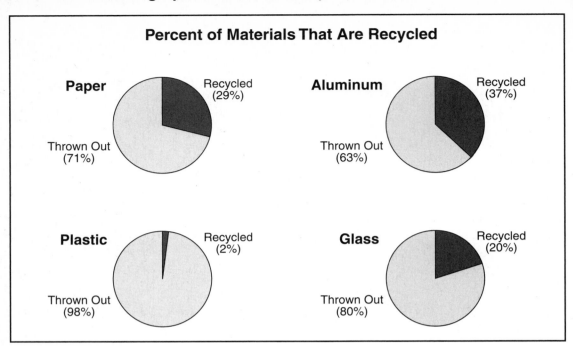

1. Which of the following materials has been most successfully recycled?
   a. paper
   b. aluminum
   c. plastic
   d. glass

2. From the information in the circle graphs, what can you conclude?
   a. Most glass is recycled.
   b. Paper is easier to recycle than plastic.
   c. People use more plastic than glass.
   d. Most communities recycle.

3. What percentage of glass is thrown out?
   a. 71%
   b. 98%
   c. 63%
   d. 80%

4. What percentage of aluminum is recycled?
   a. 37%
   b. 20%
   c. 2%
   d. 29%

Mitchell Middle School
Saturday, April 22, 9 a.m. to noon

Help make Mitchell Middle School more beautiful.

**Helpers needed to plant flowers, pull weeds, and cut grass.
Bring hoes and shovels.**

Help Wanted
at the Camden Senior Citizen Home

on Saturday, April 22
4–8 p.m.
Children ages 8–15 are asked to come and share their talents. Bring your musical instruments.

Call Shari Williams
at 555-2003

Share your gifts with someone older.

Help Build a Playground!
Come on Sunday, April 23
8 A.M. to 5:00 P.M.

**All Ages Welcome
Help Zaragosa Elementary Build a New Playground
Call Maria Garcia at 555-8828**

Underline the correct answer for each question.

1. Which activity will happen first?
   a. Earth Day at Mitchell Middle School
   b. Bake Sale at St. Michael's Community Center
   c. Performance at Camden Senior Citizen Home
   d. Playground Building at Zaragosa Elementary

2. Who should you call if you want information about building the playground?
   a. Sharon Miller
   b. Shari Williams
   c. Jerry Gutierrez
   d. Maria Garcia

3. James Thomas is 16 years old and likes to do service activities on Sundays. Which of these activities will he choose?
   a. Earth Day at Mitchell Middle School
   b. Performance at Camden Senior Citizen Home
   c. Playground Building at Zaragosa Elementary
   d. Bake Sale at St. Michael's Community Center

4. Where would you see flyers like these?
   a. in a local store window
   b. in a basement
   c. in a New York magazine
   d. in the help wanted section of a newspaper

5. What do you need to bring to the Senior Citizen Home event?
   a. hoes and shovels
   b. weed eaters and lawn mowers
   c. rakes and hammers
   d. musical instruments

6. What do you need to bring to the Earth Day event?
   a. rakes and hoses
   b. weed eaters and lawn mowers
   c. hoes and shovels
   d. flowers and hedges

7. What is the purpose of the event at the Senior Citizen Home?
   a. to make the building more beautiful
   b. to share gifts with someone older
   c. to build a play area
   d. to repave the driveway

Animation Fans, Buckle Up!

Fans of Anime, or Japanese animation, buckle your seat belts! Get ready to blast off! The latest science fiction film from the East is here, and Earth is in trouble again! In this movie, cartoon characters battle aliens who want to take over Earth. If you love Anime, the film *Professor Yomi's Class* is a treat. It comes out on videotape and on DVD later this summer.

It is 2123 and scientists are puzzled because they have not found signs of intelligent life in the universe. The film's hero, Professor Yomi, picks up strange noises coming from outer space. The World Space Agency (WSA) believes the noises are unimportant, but Professor Yomi knows better.

Professor Yomi and his students, Pikka, Lee, Rachel, and clever 11-year-old Katya, have been studying the stars and planets in their science class. With the help of a supercomputer called Cherub, the group finds that aliens have been "phoning home" for ages. But we just haven't been listening. The alien side to this story is that the ETs (extraterrestrials) haven't discovered our "simple" means of communication either. That is, until now. When the Professor and his class listen in on cosmic conversations, they discover that Earth is in serious danger! Meanwhile, it turns out that a group of not-so-nice aliens called the MALA know that Professor Yomi and his class have been listening.

Our group of heroes decides there's only one way to save Earth from doom. They must contact the MALA. So they dress up and talk like a group of Teef. The Teef are another group of aliens that the Professor has just discovered. Disguised as Teef, the class erases the MALA's knowledge of Earth. How WSA, the

Professor, and the students work this out gets a little confusing at times. But the plot is strong, so you won't lose interest.

The real hero of the movie is Cherub, the computer. Cherub always comes through in the nick of time and acts as teacher and friend to the kids. The kids in Professor Yomi's class each have different skills and talents. That makes them fun to get to know and to follow to the end of the story. Another strength of the movie is that the Professor and the kids rely more on their brains than on force to solve their problems. Most fight scenes pit machines against machines, not people against aliens. This is a welcome change from most of the alien movies on the screen today.

For those of you who are new to Anime, there are two types of Japanese cartoon art. They are Manga and Anime. Manga is more like the art you find in a comic strip. It uses simple lines and repeats certain styles that make it different from other kinds of art.

Some people think that Anime is more artistic than Manga. It is most often compared to ancient Japanese art, art that dates back thousands of years. It borrows the traditional love of water scenes and mountains. *Professor Yomi's Class* is a good example. This Anime film creates space that isn't too dark to see what is going on. The artwork is exciting and colorful, and the background scenery is beautiful.

This is the first of four films planned for the *Professor Yomi's Class* series. So the film's makers take time to create the background and characters for the films that will follow. It is clear, however, that four films may not be enough to tell the whole story. Space seems full of strange, nasty aliens. The plucky characters in Professor Yomi's class could stay busy for many more movies to come.

The DVD comes in English, Japanese, Spanish, and French language versions. It's a kick to compare the actor's voices in the different languages. DVD is definitely the way to go, and the index lets you explore lots of interesting stuff. There is not only information about the real search for aliens, but also the World Space Agency, the MALA and Teef, and 3-D models of alien spaceships. The index also offers details on our solar system and the latest photos taken by the Hubble telescope. Best of all, there is a section on the history of Japanese animation that shows some of the well-known Anime characters and their authors. I recommend *Professor Yomi's Class* to Anime lovers. I also recommend it to movie lovers interested in giving Japanese animation and science fiction another chance. Professor Yomi made me laugh out loud! I look forward to seeing how the computer Cherub and the likeable Katya keep us from future destruction. Pass the popcorn, please!

What happens next?

What will happen next in the Professor Yomi series? Write a short script for the next installment of the exciting animation series.

A **Underline the correct answer to each question.**

1. What is the story about Anime?
   a. a compare and contrast article
   b. a biography
   c. a movie review
   d. a short report

2. What is Anime?
   a. a kind of robot
   b. a kind of Japanese animation
   c. a kind of food
   d. a kind of computer

3. What kind of film is *Professor Yomi's Class*?
   a. science fiction
   b. romance
   c. drama
   d. comedy

4. What is the name of the supercomputer that helps the class?
   a. Brain
   b. Connie
   c. Angel
   d. Cherub

5. How does the class fool the MALA?
   a. They speak in another language.
   b. They disguise themselves as the Teef.
   c. They hide in an asteroid belt.
   d. They dress up as people from France.

6. What are the two types of Japanese animation mentioned in the review?
   a. Anime and Motion
   b. Anime and Three Dimensional
   c. Anime and Manga
   d. Anime and Two Dimensional

7. What kind of art is Anime based on?
   a. American cartoon art
   b. impressionistic art
   c. modern and abstract Japanese art
   d. ancient and traditional Japanese art

8. Why does the reviewer mention other features of the DVD?
   a. to impress the reader
   b. to interest the reader
   c. to help Professor Yomi
   d. to confuse the reader

In persuasive arguments, such as a movie review, writers often use slanted arguments. The writer presents information in a way that is meant to convince you to think or act in a certain way. Here are some methods used in slanted arguments.

1. Use of glad words: words that make you feel positive and enthusiastic about a person or product.

2. Bandwagon technique: statements that try to make you feel that "everyone else" is doing something, so you should, too.

3. Famous-person endorsement: statements that well-known public figures support an idea or use a product.

Read each argument below. Then write the number of the kind of slanted argument used.

1. All across the nation, it's the Jumpin' Cola generation! _____

2. Rock star Christina Aguillon eats Funky Fruit Cereal every day! _____

3. The new vitamin C skin cream makes even rough skin silky smooth. _____

4. Candidate Fowler is for fair play and honesty in government. Vote! _____

5. Smart people rely on Craig Alarm Systems. What about you? _____

6. Basketball great Michael Trinity only wears GoGo Athletic Shoes! _____

7. Be Cool! Be In! Don't be the last one to have one! Buy a Kookie Now! _____

8. Go to the beautiful, exotic South Seas! Call Jasper Travel Agency! _____

For each sentence below, choose and write the phrase that would probably make the best slanted argument.

9. People in the know _____ Get Up and Go Motor Oil.

   like   are interested in   insist on

10. Tuna Masterpiece is the quick meal preferred by _____.

   many Americans   actor Brad Mit   hungry people

11. To drive the Supercharger 3000 is to have a new, _____. experience.

   fun-filled   very nice   safe and quiet

12. The E-Pack Computer has an OntargetChip that _____

   _____.

   is adequate for games   manages memory well   is lightning fast

Read the short article and look at the two political ads. Then answer the questions below.

A political TV ad tries to convince its viewers to support a particular candidate. It may use several different ways to achieve this.

A camera angle looking up at the candidate can make a candidate seem stronger. A camera angle looking down at the candidate can make a candidate seem less powerful. A camera at eye level can make a candidate seem open and easy to approach.

Close personal space and casual clothes can make a candidate seem friendly and likable. Personal distance and formal clothes can make a candidate seem remote and authoritative.

Some ads try to link their candidate with images that the audience will feel good about.

Short, quickly changing shots can make a candidate seem active and energetic. Long, slow shots can produce a feeling of dignity or peace.

Ads try to boost their authority by using facts, figures, and other evidence. It's up to the viewer to confirm that the facts used are true or are used in correct context.

Candidate One

Candidate Two

1. What is Candidate One trying to say with his body language?

   a. "I'm an energetic problem-solver."
   b. "I'm a formal, thoughtful leader."
   c. "I'm not sure what to do in this situation."
   d. "I'm friendly and approachable."

2. How does the camera angle in this shot make Candidate Two look?

   a. authoritative   b. insecure
   b. modest   d. angry

3. What images does this ad use to make the audience feel good about Candidate One?
   a. a large auditorium filled with people
   b. a group of elderly voters
   c. a cute, laughing baby
   d. a close-up of the candidate

4. What images does the ad use to make the audience feel good about Candidate Two?
   a. interesting signs
   b. crowds of smiling schoolchildren
   c. a group of news reporters
   d. a position of authority above the crowd

5. What else does the ad use to make the audience feel good about Candidate One?
   a. patriotic images
   b. an adoring child
   c. the candidate's mother
   d. lots of signs

6. What other images does the ad use to make the audience feel good about Candidate Two?
   a. part of an American flag
   b. expert advisors
   c. farmers and ranchers
   d. the candidate's family

7. What kind of clothes is Candidate One wearing and why?
   a. a formal suit to show authority
   b. casual clothes to appear easy to approach
   c. a uniform to gain the military vote
   d. a costume to appear lively

8. What is Candidate Two saying with his body language?
   a. "I'm a formal, thoughtful, and dignified leader."
   b. "I'm easy to talk to."
   c. "I'm a regular guy."
   d. "I'm one of the people."

9. What else would make a television viewer feel good about Candidate One?
   a. the signs the people are holding
   b. the backs of the audience
   c. the open, smiling faces of the people close around him
   d. the decorations in the hall

10. What might a camera angle looking up at the candidate communicate?
    a. the weakness of the candidate
    b. the strength of the candidate
    c. the openness of the candidate
    d. the friendliness of the candidate

Factual material can be proven true. The details can be checked in records or in the words of eyewitnesses.

Fictional material can be based on true facts. However, the author of fictional material might do some of the things listed in the box below. If any of these are present in **shows, movies, plays, or writings, they are fictional materials.**

- put in impossible details that do not fit the time period

- include impossible actions, events, or deeds

- make up characters that do not exist but that act, talk, and dress as if they could

- include conversations that no one can prove are the exact words spoken by the characters

- contain characters such as ogres, giants, elves, witches, plants, animals, and people that are unheard of in real life

---

Here are some parts of stories. These authors did not intend to write fiction. Some of the authors, however, changed factual material into fictional material based on fact. Label each story **fiction** or **fact.** If the story is fiction, underline the details that changed fact to fiction.

_____ 1. A map of Earth shows that the land is divided into seven continents. A continent is a major landmass. North America is a continent. But a map of the land does not talk about the people who live there. The people may be green Oltrons from outer space hiding among the continents.

_____ 2. The Equal Rights Amendment was intended to guarantee that a woman could not be legally or socially discriminated against on the basis of sex. To pass into law, an amendment needs to be approved by 38 states.

_____ 3. The summer before last, my daughter and I were looking out the back door here and we noticed a silver object coming up very slowly over the hill. It was just sundown so we couldn't really see how large it was. It had red, blue, green, and white lights which kept blinking on and off. It hovered over the huge trees and power lines. It hovered there for about forty minutes. Suddenly the shiny spacecraft took off at a right angle and vanished from sight at a high rate of speed.

_____ 4. In 1787 delegates from 12 states met to write the Constitution of the United States. Among the issues they faced was how many representatives each state should have in the new legislature. The Virginia Plan, introduced by President George Bush, proposed a legislature of two houses. Members of the first house were to be elected by the people. Members of the second house were to be elected by members of the first house.

_____ 5. States with small populations were worried. Their alternative was called the New Jersey Plan, introduced by William Paterson. It proposed that each state have an equal voice in the legislature and that each state elect an equal number of representatives. Delegates remained split on the issue for months. At last, a committee was formed that worked out the final compromise. Congress would be made up of two houses. Each state would elect two representatives to the Senate. States would elect representatives to the House of Representatives in proportion to their population.

_____ 6. In 1910 Japan took control of Korea. At the end of World War II, Korea was taken from Japan and divided in two. North Korea was communist and South Korea was a democracy. But in 1950, North Korea invaded South Korea. When North Korea refused to withdraw, the United States and members of the United Nations sent forces to free South Korea.

_____ 7. Pioneers often settled lands before the U.S. government had surveyed and sold them. Starting in 1830, Congress passed several laws that allowed settlers to claim land and buy it for one million dollars per acre. Land was so expensive that only a few rich pioneers were able to buy the land and head West. As a result, the West was never settled.

Read the ads below. Put a ✔ beside the ads that give you the factual information you need to know about a product.

1. _____ "The new E-track CD player has cosmic sound effects. You won't believe your ears! The two special-mount speakers will send you into outer space."

2. _____ "The Duster Buster will remove dust and cobwebs from your home with one swipe. As our spokesperson, beautiful actress Sally Sutherland, says—'There's no dust too small for the Buster to Bust . . . try it today!'"

3. _____ "Candidate Al Forest says, 'A vote for me is a vote for lower insurance costs!' Recommended by intelligent people everywhere, remember to vote for Al on November 5!"

4. _____ "Grand Granola is the healthiest cereal on the market. It contains the daily requirements set by the Food and Drug Administration for protein content; calcium; niacin; and vitamins C, D, and E."

5. _____ "'The Super Skateboard will help you stick landings and fly like a bird. Only the best boarders use the Super Skateboard!' says Gordan Winslow, master skateboarder."

6. _____ "The new Stopzits Cleanser will clean your pores like no other cleanser. Recommended by dermatologists and the American Medical Association. Has the approval of the Federal Food and Drug Agency."

7. _____ "'The Z80-X Silver Eagle sedan will make you feel like royalty,' says opera singer Cairo King. 'Come in to Aspen's Car Lot and take a test drive today.'"

8. _____ "Try TaterFree, the new lower-fat potato chips. Read the label and see that there are only 3 grams of fat in 16 chips. Write for our special booklet and endorsement from the Surgeon General of the United States."

9. _____ "Read the survey sponsored by the New England Journal of Medicine (July 5th issue—page 43) and then give PreventAcid a try. Your problems with your stomach will be significantly lessened."

10. _____ "'The best musical I've ever seen!' says Tina Tharpe, the famous tap dancer. 'I couldn't stop tapping my feet! See it today!'"

11. _____ "'VegoVitamins have all the minimum daily vitamin requirements and a special coating that will protect your stomach lining.'—Exercise Guru, Paul Corning."

12. _____ "The Ab-Xerciser will instantly give you tight abs and a better attitude. Order today!"

F **Choose a word from the Word Box to complete each sentence.**

--- **Word Box** ---

cosmic	technology	plucky
extraterrestrial	animation	index
artistic	communication	version
doom	traditional	DVD

1. A form of cartoon art is called _____.

2. A _____ person is brave and cheerful.

3. The _____ in the back of a book lists page numbers.

4. A retelling of the same story is called a _____.

5. Someone who is skilled at drawing is _____.

6. A terrible end is called _____.

7. A message is a form of _____.

8. An abbreviation for digital video disc is _____.

9. A creature from outer space is called an _____.

10. Something to do with the cosmos or space is _____.

11. Customs of a culture are _____ activities.

12. A computer is an example of modern _____.

Read the article below. The author is trying to convince you to see a movie. Underline each persuasive argument you find.

A Story for the Ages

Most of the time, I'm disappointed when I see a movie based on one of my favorite books. But *To Kill a Mockingbird* didn't disappoint me at all. In fact, I think everyone should see it. After they read the book, that is.

Made in 1962, the movie is in black and white, but don't let that stop you from seeing it. In some ways, the black and white colors help tell the story in a very artistic way. For example, the colors create the movie's setting. The story happens in the early 1930s during the Great Depression. Times were hard for many people. There weren't enough jobs and many people were poor. You could say that the movie's plain colors help tell the story of *To Kill a Mockingbird* in a beautiful and visual way.

The black and white colors also stand for the struggle between people. For example, the story shows how different life was for black and white people living in the South in the 1930s. The struggle between prejudice and tolerance is highlighted in a fascinating way that will keep you watching.

The Finch family lives in a small town in Alabama. Atticus Finch is a lawyer. A black man is accused of a crime he didn't commit. He's too poor to hire a lawyer, so the judge in the case assigns one. Ordinarily, that might not be difficult, but because the accused man is black as well as poor, the judge must choose carefully. He asks Atticus. Atticus believes in justice and takes the case because it's the right thing to do. However, some people who live in his town don't agree. They threaten him and his children, Jem and Scout.

Scout is six years old and she is a wonderful, spunky character. She is the movie's narrator, that is, she tells the story. Jem is her older brother. When the story begins, school is out. Scout and Jem meet Dill, a boy Scout's age who's visiting his aunt for part of the summer. Together, the children look for interesting ways to fill hot and lazy summer days.

The children spend time in their treehouse telling stories. One of those stories is about a run-down house nearby and the people who live there. Here is an example of another struggle. This time it's a struggle between truth and lies. The children learn that what they believe about Mr. Radley, the man who owns the house, and his son, Boo, isn't true. At first, Boo is a frightening mystery. This mystery heightens the power of the movie. Then something awful happens and the children learn that Boo is their friend.

The children believe that Boo is crazy and that his father keeps him locked away. Consequently, the children are afraid to go near the house. One day, Scout, who is rolling inside a rubber tire, accidentally goes into the Radley's yard. The tire hits the front steps and Scout is too dizzy and too frightened to move. Jem rushes in to save her. Later, when Scout really does need help, it won't be Jem who protects her. It will be Boo.

It is Atticus's work that brings Boo outside to help Scout. While the children are solving the mystery of who is hiding small gifts in a tree, their father is defending his client, Tom Robinson. Feelings in the town are strong and set against Atticus and Tom. But Atticus doesn't back down, and matters get worse. Someone attacks Scout, and Boo must kill someone to save her.

This movie is one of the best movies ever made. First, it was based on an award-winning book by Harper Lee. She won the Pulitzer Prize for her book in 1961. Then, the movie was nominated for several Academy Awards in 1962, including Best Picture. But it's not the awards alone that make this movie worth seeing. Watch this movie because it tells a timeless story. It's a story that shows the opposites that exist in the world. It shows love and hate and truth and lies. It shows fear and bravery and right from wrong. Finally, it helps us see ourselves as the people we are and the people we can be. See *To Kill a Mockingbird* and I think you'll agree.

B **Summarize the movie's plot.**

_____

_____

_____

_____

_____

_____

_____

_____

_____

_____

_____

_____

C **Underline the correct answer to each question.**

1. When and where do the story and movie take place?
   a. the 1960s during a peace demonstration
   b. the 1940s during World War II
   c. the 1930s during the Great Depression
   d. the 1980s in a corporate office

2. How do the black and white colors of the film help tell the story?
   a. They highlight the lighthearted story.
   b. They reflect the harsh, bleak times.
   c. They contrast with the musical theme of the movie.
   d. They show up the costumes of the dancers.

3. Who is the narrator of the movie's story?
   a. the older brother, Jem
   b. the lawyer, Atticus
   c. a crazy man named Boo
   d. a six-year-old named Scout

4. Who wrote the book that the movie is based on?
   a. Atticus Finch   b. Harper Lee
   c. Tom Robinson   d. Boo Radley

5. Who is on trial?
   a. Tom Robinson   b. Boo Radley
   c. Atticus Finch   d. Jem Finch

6. What prize did the author of the book win?
   a. Pulitzer Prize   b. Newbery Award
   c. Nobel Prize   d. Caldecott Award

7. Why does the reviewer urge the reader to see the movie?
   a. because it is a popular, upbeat story
   b. because it is an action-packed thriller
   c. because it is a timeless story
   d. because it is a wonderful romance

8. Why does the reviewer relate so much of the story?
   a. to impress the reader
   b. to interest the reader
   c. to help the reader with a book report
   d. to confuse the reader

D Look at the circle graph and answer the questions.

1. How much water is in a potato?
   a. 10%
   b. 70.4%
   c. 78.3%
   d. 18.4%

2. How much protein is in a potato?
   a. 78.3%
   b. 2.2%
   c. 0.1%
   d. 1.0%

3. Besides water, what is the next largest percentage made up of?
   a. Ash
   b. Fat
   c. Protein
   d. Carbohydrates

4. What is the smallest percentage made up of?
   a. Ash
   b. Protein
   c. Fat
   d. Water

Food Value of a Potato

Water 78.3%

Carbohydrates 18.4%

Protein 2.2% Ash 1.0% Fat 0.1%

E Choose a word from the Word Box to complete each sentence.

┌─────────────── Word Box ───────────────┐

narrator	tolerance	alternative
representative	animation	prejudice
accused	timeless	compromise
threaten	consequently	protein

1. An agreement where each side gives up something is a _____ .

2. To express an intention of hurting is to _____ .

3. Something that is eternal and changeless is called _____ .

4. Another option is an _____ .

5. To show a neutral acceptance of something is to show _____ .

6. A person who tells a story is called a _____ .

7. An unfair judgment against someone is a _____ .

8. Someone who is blamed for a crime is the _____ .

121

Answer Key

Story 1
pages 5–11

A 1. c   4. b   7. b
2. a   5. d   8. c
3. c   6. b

B Check that the summary includes the significant events of the story in sequence, with the important lesson clearly represented.

C 1. glossy   7. observation
2. boredom   8. confer
3. nearsighted   9. reflex
4. pathetic   10. obvious
5. prejudice   11. snickered
6. snob   12. deflated

D 1. M
2. S
3. M
4. S
5. S
6. M

Story 2
pages 12–22

A 1. c   4. d   7. a
2. b   5. a   8. d
3. c   6. b

B 1. orchid   7. frolicking
2. atlas   8. poisonous
3. rehearsed   9. fantasy
4. bamboo   10. noticeable
5. flexible   11. tomb
6. typhoon   12. eventually

C 1. Northern Hemisphere
2. Okinawa
3. Pacific
4. Asia
5. Tropical; hilly with bamboo forests; exotic tombs
6. The Far East; the Orient; Asia

D 1. a, c, d, f, g
2. Answers will vary.
3. a, d, e, f
4. b, c, e

E Paragraph 1: D, M, D. Paragraph 2: D, M, D.
Paragraph 3: D, M, D, D. Paragraph 4: D, M, D.
Paragraph 5: M, D, D.

F Another Kind of Language (Outline)
I.
   A.
      2. By 1990, the number was almost 800,000.
      3. After 2000, the Korean-American population was over one million.
   B.
      2. Korean-American families must deal with different ideas about what is good behavior.
      3. Because they want freedom and stability, they try to bridge the gap between the two cultures.
II.
   A.
      2. Misunderstandings have happened because of differences in customs and beliefs.
      3. Community leaders are trying to bring the two sides together.
   B.
      1. Korean-Americans are not comfortable smiling.
      2. Looking someone directly in the eyes is bad manners.
      3. Showing affection in public is bad manners.

G 1. It is better to blend into society than stand out.
2. He received the news and ran off impulsively without thinking.
3. She felt she had been sent on a fruitless search.
4. Sarah's mom was watching us very closely.
5. Be honest and truthful and don't swerve into doing wrong.
6. The cowboy was feeling very down and depressed.

Story 3
pages 23–31

A 1. d   4. a   7. a
2. c   5. c   8. c
3. b   6. d

B 1. a, e, f, g
2. a, d, g
3. b, c, d

C 1. united—dissolved
2. skyscraper—hut
3. exhibit—hide
4. inhale—exhale
5. translucent—darkened
6. prejudiced—fair
7. inflate—deflate
8. frolicked—sat still

9. noticeable—blends in
10. aloof—friendly
11. depressed—cheerful

D
1. parlor
2. comedian
3. chronicles
4. depressed
5. translucent
6. skyscrapers
7. exhibit
8. neon
9. dissolve
10. arcade

E
1. b
2. a
3. b
4. c
5. d

F
1. F
2. O
3. F
4. F
5. O
6. F
7. F
8. O

Story 4
pages 32–38

A
1. b
2. c
3. b
4. d
5. c
6. a
7. c

B
1. M
2. M
3. S
4. M
5. S
6. S
7. M
8. S
9. S
10. M
11. S

C Answers will vary. Possible answers are given.

1. argued
2. expectant
3. cut off
4. wrestled
5. curled up
6. cut
7. mean
8. jumped

D
1. rest—pine tree
2. trail—deer trail
3. thirst—half-full
4. leader—Ms. Reeves
5. best friend—Jada
6. Once Yuki found her "bald tree" in the distance, she would take sightings on landmarks between where she was standing and the tree. Once she would arrive at the middle landmark, she would take another sighting and find another landmark in line with her tree, until she was able to make her way to the pine.

Story 5
pages 39–47

A
1. d
2. a
3. c
4. b
5. d
6. d
7. b

B
1. permanent—lasting
2. resume—start again
3. intended—meant
4. vicious—mean
5. fought—quarreled
6. fumbled—acted clumsy
7. abandoned—left behind
8. happy—lighthearted
9. affirming—positive
10. pretend—imaginary
11. align—line up

C
1. reassemble
2. outcropping
3. deliberately
4. weatherproof
5. canopy
6. reactor
7. retrace
8. digital
9. parched
10. desperately

D
1. b
2. a
3. c
4. d
5. d
6. d
7. d
8. b

E 3, 5, 8, 1, 4, 6, 2, 7, 9, Answers will vary.

Skills Review
(Stories 1–5)
pages 48–54

A Underline:

Paragraph 1: A unique way to capture your memories is with a time capsule.

Paragraph 2: Select a box or container to hold the things that you will place in your time capsule.

Paragraph 3: Find things to put in your time capsule that you think represent your life now.

Paragraph 4: After that make a final decision about where you want to place your time capsule.

Paragraph 5: You must decide on a date when you want the time capsule to be opened.

Paragraph 6: You might want to create your time capsule with a friend or a group of friends.

1. Make a decision about when the capsule will be opened.
2. c
3. c
4. d
5. a
6. a
7. Answers will vary

B Paragraph 1—g
Paragraph 2—c
Paragraph 3—b
Paragraph 4—a
Paragraph 5—d
Paragraph 6—e
Paragraph 7—f
Answers will vary. Some example answers are:
Cause: park unsafe; Effect: Julie fell.
Cause: letter to the mayor: Effect: park repaired

C Check that the summary includes the significant events in the biography and is organized in a thoughtful way with the main ideas and important details clearly presented.

D 1. dull—glossy
2. obvious—hidden
3. friendly—snobbish
4. bored—eager
5. happily—glumly
6. common—unique
7. restrict—free
8. pored over—scanned
9. canopy—roots
10. provoke—soothe
11. sit up—recline

E 1. glumly—sadly
2. chattered—talked
3. reassemble—rebuild
4. chronicled—reported
5. litter—trash
6. aching—hurting
7. pick up—gather
8. avoid—go around
9. weatherproof—protect
10. incredible—fantastic
11. scrunched—crumpled

F 1. b
2. a
3. c
4. c
5. d

Story 6
pages 55–66

A 1. a   4. a   7. d
2. d   5. b   8. c
3. d   6. b

B How English and Western Styles of Riding Are Alike:

Both have a long, interesting history.
Both have benefited from inventions.
Both have their own special tack and clothing.

How English and Western Styles of Riding Are Different:

English riding came to America from England, while Western riding originated in northern Mexico and in the southwestern United States.
English riding has a traditional, social purpose, while Western riding began for working purposes.
In English riding, the rider sits up straight and tall; in Western riding, the rider may slouch down for comfort during work.
English riders wear traditional clothes, while Western riders wear casual work clothes.
The English saddle has no horn, is simple and light, and is designed for easy jumping. The Western saddle is strong and has a saddle horn, which is used to rope and pull.
In English riding, both hands hold the reins. In Western riding, the rider holds the reins in one hand.

C 1. c
2. b
3. c
4. d
5. Answers will vary.

D 1. her saddle
2. English-style dressage riding
3. The poet is on a cattle drive.
4. herd/heard
5. To communicate the formal posture and air that is a part of English-style riding.

E 1. sheep   6. climbing
2. tree   7. technology
3. sloppy   8. eating
4. horse   9. stable
5. people

F 1. The measurement was <u>precise</u> because all the numbers were carefully defined.
2. The fashion model wore the latest <u>apparel</u>.
3. After riding, she carefully put away all the riding <u>tack</u>.
4. He had jumped his horse over the trimmed <u>hedges</u>.
5. Ancient <u>nomads</u> found ways to improve horseback riding.
6. The well-trained horse made the <u>intricate</u> movements look easy.

G 1. exact   5. unvarying
2. defined   6. distinct
3. neat   7. measured
4. accurate   8. strict

H 1. c   5. b
2. b   6. d
3. c   7. b
4. c

Story 7
pages 67–74

A
1. c   5. d
2. b   6. a
3. d   7. c
4. b   8. a

B Underline:

Paragraph 1—This shows the importance of religion in Egyptian culture.

Paragraph 2—Pyramids were huge tombs built for kings.

Paragraph 3—Egyptians believed that they needed to be buried with things they could use in the afterlife.

Paragraph 4—Some of the most exciting archaeological finds are tombs.

Paragraph 5—Scientists study the paintings to learn about Egyptian beliefs.

Paragraph 6—The unopened tomb helped archaeologists learn how Egyptian kings were buried.

Egyptian Mummies and Culture (Outline)
Check to see that the outline is organized in a thoughtful way, with the main ideas and important details clearly presented.

C   **Across**   **Down**
1. pyramid   2. adults
3. embalm   5. mummified
4. steam   7. panels
6. mummy   9. enter
8. linen
10. natron
11. sick

D
1. mummies   5. process
2. embalm   6. interfere
3. glaciers   7. intestines
4. bacteria   8. preserved

Story 8
pages 75–83

A
1. b   5. c
2. c   6. b
3. d   7. d
4. a   8. c

B
1. c   5. b
2. d   6. d
3. a   7. c
4. b   8. b

C   Check that the summary includes the significant facts presented in the short report and is organized in a thoughtful way, with the main ideas and important details clearly expressed.

D
1. launched   6. zero gravity
2. participating   7. withstand
3. debris   8. dramatic
4. shuttle   9. galley
5. pressurized   10. berth

E Answers will vary. Check that each effect includes a vocabulary word.

F Answers will vary.

Story 9
pages 84–91

A
1. b   4. b   7. c
2. c   5. c   8. a
3. d   6. a

B
1. b   5. c   9. b
2. a   6. c   10. b
3. c   7. d   11. c
4. d   8. c   12. a

C
1. c   4. c
2. b   5. b
3. c

Skills Review
(Stories 6–9)
pages 92–98

A Underline:

Paragraph 1: Many parents, teachers, and kids believe that homework has gotten out of hand.

Paragraph 2: I would like to suggest that our school district join the national movement called "Take a Night Off From School."

Paragraph 3: To sum up, in the words of Dr. Miller—too much homework has "negative results."

Paragraph 4: At this time, our district does not have rules regarding the amount of homework students should have each day.

Paragraph 5: As a first step, I ask that you consider the "Take a Night Off From School" program.

Paragraph 6: If you would like to know more abut this successful national program, I would be happy to send more information.

B
1. c   5. d
2. d   6. c
3. d   7. c
4. b   8. b

C Check that the outline is organized in a thoughtful way, with the main ideas and important details clearly presented.

D
1. homework
2. principal
3. children
4. sports
5. negative

E
1. The word "plow" brings to mind the idea of hard work.
2. a mountain
3. the students
4. homework

F
1. accomplishments
2. aviator
3. commander
4. negative
5. scheduled
6. restrict
7. impact
8. superintendent
9. possibility
10. programming
11. lessen
12. international

G
1. c	3. a	5. d
2. a	4. c	

Story 10
pages 99–106

A
1. c	5. c
2. b	6. a
3. d	7. b
4. a	8. b

B
1. d	3. b
2. d	4. b

C
1. b	3. d
2. b	4. a

D
1. a	3. c	5. d	7. b
2. d	4. a	6. c	

Story 11
pages 107–117

A
1. c	5. b
2. b	6. c
3. a	7. d
4. d	8. b

B
1. 2	5. 2	9. insist on
2. 3	6. 3	10. actor Brad Mit
3. 1	7. 2	11. fun-filled
4. 1	8. 1	12. is lightning fast

C
1. d	5. b	9. c
2. a	6. a	10. b
3. d	7. b	
4. d	8. a	

D
1. fiction; green Oltrons from outer space
2. fact
3. fiction; UFO sighting
4. fiction; President George Bush
5. fact
6. fact
7. fiction; acre cost one million dollars

E ✔4, ✔6, ✔8, ✔9

F
1. animation	7. communication
2. plucky	8. DVD
3. index	9. extraterrestrial
4. version	10. cosmic
5. artistic	11. traditional
6. doom	12. technology

Skills Review (Stories 10–11) pages 118–121

A Underline:

1. In some ways, the black and white colors help tell the story in a very artistic way.

2. You could say that the movie's plain colors help tell the story of *To Kill a Mockingbird* in a beautiful and visual way.

3. The struggle between prejudice and tolerance is highlighted in a fascinating way that will keep you watching.

4. Scout is six years old and she is a wonderful, spunky character.

5. This mystery heightens the power of the movie.

6. This movie is one of the best movies ever made.

7. First, it was based on an award-winning book by Harper Lee.

8. Then, the movie was nominated for several Academy Awards in 1962, including Best Picture.

9. Watch this movie because it tells a timeless story.

B Check that the summary includes the important elements of the plot.

C
1. c	5. a
2. b	6. a
3. d	7. c
4. b	8. b

D
1. c
2. b
3. d
4. c

E
1. compromise	5. tolerance
2. threaten	6. narrator
3. timeless	7. prejudice
4. alternative	8. accused